THE GREATEST SHORTSTOPS OF ALL TIME

THE GREATEST SHORTSTOPS OF ALL TIME

Donald Honig

Brown &
Benchmark

For my daughter, Cathy

ACKNOWLEDGMENTS

For assistance in gathering the photographs used in this book, the author would like to express his appreciation to Patricia Kelly and her spirited colleagues at the National Baseball Hall of Fame and Museum at Cooperstown, New York; and to Michael P. Aronstein of TV Sports Mailbag.

Gratitude must also be expressed to Tom Heitz and Bill Deane, librarian and chief research assistant, respectively, of the National Baseball Hall of Fame Museum, for sharing with the author their vast knowledge of baseball history. The author is also appreciative of help received from Steve Gietschier, Archivist of *The Sporting News*, and the astute consultation of Stanley Honig, David Markson, Lawrence Ritter, Jeffrey Neuman, and George Sullivan.

The Donald Honig
Best Players of All Time Series

Cover design by Andy Nelson

Interior design by Kay D. Fulton

Copyright © 1992 by Wm. C. Brown Communications, Inc. All rights reserved

Library of Congress Catalog Card Number: 91–61839

ISBN 0-697-13505-5

Printed in the United States of America by Wm. C. Brown Publishers, 2460 Kerper Boulevard, Dubuque, IA 52001

10 9 8 7 6 5 4 3 2 1

By Donald Honig

CONTENTS

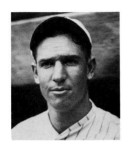

INTRODUCTION

An old axiom says "never apologize, never explain." And so, when compiling a list for baseball fans of the "best" or "greatest," one need not apologize, but may certainly have to explain.

In choosing the great first basemen, hitting is the foremost consideration. In choosing the great shortstops, however, the demands of the position must be given judicious thought. The position of shortstop demands a player whose primary talent is defense, and therefore the position may justify a weak hitter. Yet, some hitting may be too feathery, and so a .228 lifetime batting average forces one of the position's acknowledged defensive masters, Mark Belanger, to be taken off the top list. On the other hand, one of the hardest-hitting of all shortstops, Vern Stephens, was regarded as having been simply "adequate" in the field. Again a fatal flaw for a list as abbreviated as this book presents.

It takes imposing skills to play shortstop in the big leagues. The merest errant moment is almost always costly. At the corners, even at second base, a player can juggle a hard-hit ball and still recover in time to throw the runner out. But, at shortstop, because of the amount of ground to cover and the length of the throw to first base, the slightest bobble or misjudgment can leave the runner safe.

Because of the range demanded of the shortstop, this player is often called "the center fielder of the infield." The shortstop has to be inordinately quick in breaking right or left and must be able to throw from deep in the hole, as well as charge the meandering ground ball and scoop and throw while on the run. Strength of arm and accuracy of throw are basic to the job.

The shortstop must have the agility to make a double play and get out of the way before a baserunner comes along, and a certain hardiness for those times when a sliding baserunner cannot be avoided.

Perhaps the shortstop's most spectacular skill is throwing from midair while being upended in the midst of a double play.

Given the crucial nature of the position, few successful teams have been able to dominate without a highly skilled man at shortstop. Consequently, there have been many extremely gifted players at the post designated "number 6." Selecting the best is difficult and, at times, seems almost arbitrary. The quality of the players mentioned in the "And Not Forgetting . . ." chapter at the end of the book will bear this out.

THE GREATEST SHORTSTOPS OF ALL TIME

Honus Wagner.

National Baseball Library, Cooperstown, NY.

HONUS WAGNER

With the exception of Babe Ruth, no baseball player's reputation has existed with greater security than Honus Wagner's. As with Ruth, there is a rare and perfect blend of fact and myth in Wagner's career. His story is so compelling and winning that Wagner has remained safe from skeptics, doubters, and revisionists.

Wagner was the greatest shortstop of all time: that is one of baseball's few unchallenged pronouncements. He straddles the position like a colossus. There is no one remotely close. (Baseball's second greatest shortstop would be the more vigorous debate.) Some believe Wagner was the champion of all baseball players, which historically means he surpasses Ruth and Ty Cobb.

On a ball field, there was nothing Wagner couldn't do, and do wondrously. Before becoming a full-time shortstop, Honus Wagner played and excelled at first and third bases, and in the outfield.

Wagner could hit (.329 lifetime average, National League record eight batting championships), and in the dead ball era he hit hard (651 doubles, 252 triples). He could run (720 stolen bases). And his defensive play, which included a throwing arm like a Howitzer was legendary. If Wagner's manifold physical gifts were not enough, nature had also provided him with a keen baseball sense. As one writer stated in a 1914 article: "He plays almost by instinct and his instinct is unerring. Such players know intuitively what others must learn. They already possess the power of mind to act instantly and correctly. They know almost without thinking what is the proper thing to do and the proper way to do it."

Wagner's on-the-field miracles of speed and power were performed despite a physique that seemed the antithesis of an athlete's. At an inch under six feet tall and weighing 200 pounds, he was a bulky man, big shouldered, barrel-chested, long-armed (someone joked that he could tie his shoelaces without bending over), and bow-legged. When in full flight around the bases, it was said he resembled a speedily spinning hoop.

● *Wagner (right) shaking hands with Napoleon Lajoie.*

Wagner's personality remains vivid and fresh to this day. Quiet, modest, and folksy, he possessed a magnetism that riveted his contemporaries and fascinated fans, even generations after his heyday. While Napoleon Lajoie, a stellar American League second baseman and contemporary of Wagner's, hit harder than Wagner and played with a grace the Dutchman lacked, today Lajoie is but a page in the record book. Wagner, on the other hand, remains a "character," elevated to a special pantheon that includes Ruth, Cobb, and Walter Johnson.

Ruth was the gargantuan slugger, a roistering man with an unlimited appetite for life; Cobb was the snarling overachiever, evoking fear and respect; Johnson was the pitcher of quiet dignity and breathtaking speed. And then there was Wagner, the homespun philosopher and crackerbarrel storyteller.

"Once," Wagner said, "I was sent up to pinch-hit in the bottom of the ninth with the score tied. I hit the ball over the fence, but I got so excited I started running the bases the wrong way—up the third base line and all the way around back to home plate. When I touched the plate the umpire subtracted a run and we lost."

On another occasion, the solemn Wagner averred, "I was about to field a ground ball when a rabbit ran in front of me. In my haste I picked up the rabbit and threw it to first base. Got the runner by a hare."

But the folksiness seemed to conceal depths of melancholy. A writer who spent some time with him once wrote that there was "a tinge of sadness in his face. He has chosen to wrap his thoughts, his very personality, in that veil of unobtrusive sadness, and it is little wonder that the broken glimpses of his real personality which show beneath that veil should be oddly variant and contradictory. Generous in his own peculiar way, kindly and considerate, shrewd in business and yet strikingly regardless of money, eccentric in his manner, silent, taciturn and brilliant, shunning companionship even with his fellows, and yet universally popular, Wagner is a national character, the prodigy of the diamond, the grand old man of baseball."

This American original was born on February 24, 1874, at Mansfield (later Carnegie),

Pennsylvania, not far from Pittsburgh. The robust youngster, John Peter Wagner, was one of nine children of a Bavarian-born immigrant who hacked out a living in the coal mines of western Pennsylvania. The nickname "Honus" was derived from "Johannes" or "Johann," the German equivalents of "John." If not for his skills at America's sunshine game, young John Peter would have followed his father down the shafts and along the sunless underground tunnels. And he did for awhile, at the age of twelve, when he worked loading a ton of coal a day for a weekly wage of $3.50.

Unlike most immigrants, who frowned upon their sons "wasting" their time playing frivolous games, Papa Wagner liked baseball and encouraged his sons to play. Honus's older brother Albert was also interested in baseball and played one year in the National League in 1898.

In 1895, the twenty-one-year-old Honus entered professional baseball. In his first year, he played for four different teams in four different leagues in Ohio and Michigan, batting .402 in one league and over .360 in the others. In those days, minor leagues frequently folded, and at the end of the season, Wagner was a free agent.

His many talents, however, had not gone unnoticed or uncelebrated. Reports of his skills came to the attention of Ed Barrow, who would later manage the Boston Red Sox and convert Babe Ruth from pitcher to outfielder, and then move into the New York Yankees front office where, as farm director and, subsequently, as general manager, he helped build the team's dynastic success.

Barrow was 27 years old in 1895 and had just acquired the Paterson, New Jersey, club of the newly organized Atlantic League. Intrigued by the reports about Wagner, Barrow set out for western Pennsylvania to sign the young man to a contract.

Barrow arrived in Mansfield on a raw autumn day and upon getting off the train began inquiring about young John Peter Wagner. The visitor was eventually directed to the freight

● *Ed Barrow around the time he "discovered" Wagner.*
National Baseball Library, Cooperstown, NY.

yards where, he was told, he might find Wagner with some friends. Buttoning up his overcoat and firming his derby on his head, Barrow bent into the harsh winds and began walking, not knowing he was heading down the high road into baseball history.

As he related the story years later, Barrow said that as he approached the yards, he began to hear a series of resounding knocks, like stones crashing into a hollow metal. When he came upon the scene of the noise, he saw the cause was not stones but pieces of coal, being hurled against the sides of an empty hopper car by a group of young men.

● *Wagner scoring a tough run at New York's old polo grounds. Note that shin guards were not yet standard equipment for catchers, which dates this photo as sometime before 1910.*

Unseen, Barrow stood and watched. It didn't take long for him to notice the one young man with a rather bulky body, who swung gracefully before releasing the piece of coal, firing it in a blurring line toward the hopper car where it boomed loudly. That was a ballplayer's arm. Barrow knew he had stumbled upon a bit of talent, in fact, as he would often state in the next half century, more talent than he would ever see again.

The historic moment was not without its comic element. When the young men spotted the stranger watching them, they thought he was a railroad detective and began to run away. Barrow chased after them through the railroad yards, yelling that he was Edward Barrow and that he was looking for John Peter Wagner the ballplayer.

"We ran like the dickens," Wagner recalled years later, "but when he kept calling my name I figured I'd better stop."

When Barrow returned home, signed contract in pocket, he knew at least two things about his new acquisition: the boy had a strong arm and could "run like the dickens."

It didn't take long before Barrow found out the boy could also hit, as well as play just about any position on the field. Playing first, third, and the outfield for Paterson in 1896, Wagner batted .349. Midway through the next season he was batting .379. Then Barrow sold him to the Louisville club, which was in the National League at that time. The rookie broke into 61 games and batted .344.

After the 1899 season, the National League cut back from twelve teams to eight. One of the cities dropped from the league was Louisville, and fourteen players—virtually the entire squad—were transferred to the Pittsburgh Pirates. Wagner was delighted with the move, for it brought him close to home.

● *A rather dapper Honus posing with a couple of his hunting dogs.*
National Baseball Library, Cooperstown, NY.

In 1900, one year before the formation of the American League, Wagner won the first of his eight batting titles. Winning it on the final day of the season, he later described it as "the greatest kick I ever got out of baseball." It was the best offensive year of his career, as he achieved personal highs in batting (.381), triples (22), slugging (.573), and hits (201). All but his hit total were league-leading figures.

In these early years, he was still being posted all over the field and performing so proficiently at each position that one writer, when asked to list the best defensive players in the league by position, entered Wagner's name for first base, third base, and outfield.

It wasn't until Wagner became a full-time shortstop in 1903 that his reputation began to reach new heights.

● *Tommy Leach.*

"Nobody had ever seen the position played like that, and that's the truth," said Pirate third baseman Tommy Leach, who played alongside Honus for ten years. "No shortstop had ever had his range, his quickness, and his arm. For a man of his size, you couldn't believe how fast he could move, and with those long arms and big hands he could stop just about anything."

Part of the Wagner legend was the image of Honus scooping up handfuls of dirt and pebbles along with the entrapped baseball and firing the whole mélange to first base.

"That was true," Leach said. "I never saw any other infielder do that. It was the size of his hands, you see. When he swept the ball into his

glove it was like a vacuum cleaner taking everything around it, and then when he grabbed the ball out of the glove, those big fingers just cleaned everything else out and fired it all over to first base." A Wagner peg singing across the diamond must have looked to the first baseman like some galactic object emerging from a rush of trailing satellites.

Led by their sad-faced superstar, the Pirates were the National League's dominant team in the opening years of the new century. The Pirates won pennants in 1901, 1902, and 1903, and in 1903, the team had the distinction of representing the National League in the first World Series ever played. The Pirates lost to Boston, and Honus did not fare too well, batting just .222 and committing six errors. He would not see the inside of another World Series until 1909.

Beginning in 1903, Wagner won seven batting championships in nine years and, along the way, set a record by winning three RBI titles in three consecutive years (1907–09). If Wagner's fielding and speed afoot (he led in stolen bases five times) never ceased to dazzle, then his hitting was especially impressive. As shortstop Joe Tinker of the celebrated Chicago Cubs double play unit said, "Shortstops, as a rule, don't hit very well." However, Tinker said:

"To me the most remarkable thing about Wagner is that he has played shortstop for so many years and still has batted as he has. If Ty Cobb, for instance, had played short and had got spiked as many times as he probably would have been, it is a grave question in my mind if he wouldn't have hit at least fifty points less than he had done in the outfield, where there is comparatively little to do and a player has about all his energy left to devote to batting and baserunning. Wagner has gone on year after year at the most difficult position in the game, and at the same time has led his league eight times in batting, and has always been a star baserunner."

Wagner lived by his own singular code of ethics, which included an apparent indifference to money. When the American League was gearing up in 1901, with those gears oiled to purring by money, Wagner turned down dollars many times his annual salary of $2,400 in Pittsburgh. In 1909 he attained a peak salary of $10,000 and was content, never asking for an increase and routinely signing for the same amount year after year. Something of a loner, he lived quietly in a modest house, surrounded by his hunting dogs. He did not marry until he was forty years old.

Though he liked to drink beer, Wagner never touched hard liquor, and though he enjoyed cigars, he frowned upon cigarettes. Once a tobacco company began giving away baseball cards in cigarette packages. The series included a likeness of Wagner, but Honus objected so strenuously to being associated with cigarettes, he threatened legal action if the offending cards were not withdrawn. The company complied, destroying the cards; but a few survived, and today they are the crème de la crème for baseball card collectors. According to some price guidelines, these cards are worth as much as $400,000 a piece.

Against the Detroit Tigers, in his second and final World Series in 1909, Honus took the field against his only rival at the top of the game's pantheon, Ty Cobb. It was a match, in the words of one writer, between "the antelope and the buffalo." Though Wagner disdained personal rivalries, he still possessed the keen competitive pride that is the eternal flame of any great athlete.

"Honus didn't say much about the rivalry with Cobb," Pirate catcher George Gibson said, "but it was all over the papers. You would have thought it was Wagner versus Cobb instead of Pittsburgh versus Detroit. When I mentioned it to him, Honus just smiled. I could tell he was determined to play the sharpest ball he could, even if he didn't say it."

Pittsburgh won the Series in seven games, and the "buffalo" played rings around the "antelope." Where Cobb batted just .231 and stole

● *Wagner and Cobb (right) during the 1909 World Series.*
National Baseball Library, Cooperstown, NY.

two bases, Wagner batted .333 and stole six. Plus, Wagner was in Gibson's words, "showing the world how shortstop was to be played."

Wagner continued playing beyond his prime. After 17 straight seasons of .300 or better, he began to slip in 1914, batting .252. Yet he still spent full seasons at shortstop. When pitcher Burleigh Grimes, who came to the big leagues as a rookie with the Pirates in 1916 and pursued his Hall of Fame career until 1934, was asked late in life who was the greatest shortstop he ever saw, Grimes said, "Wagner."

"But," his questioner said, "Wagner was forty-two years old when you saw him."

"What's that got to do with it?" Grimes said. "I never saw anybody play it like he did."

Wagner finally retired after the 1917 season, leaving with 3,430 lifetime hits, a .329 batting average, and a unique place at the top of the baseball scrolls.

Wagner later rejoined the Pirates as a coach in 1933, and remained in the job until 1951, though in his later years more ornamental than anything else.

He died on December 6, 1955, at the age of seventy-nine.

During his years as a coach, Wagner would occasionally be lured onto the field during batting practice. One young Pittsburgh player recalled what it was like:

"He didn't do it often, but when he did, it was something to see. First you'd see the other infielders move away from him, far away, almost as if they didn't think they belonged out there with him. Everybody would go on with what they were doing, but they were watching him out of the corners of their eyes, and as soon as a ball was hit his way, by God, everybody froze and watched him pick it up and arc a soft, lazy throw over to first base. Then we'd look back at each other and everybody had a little smile on his face. Something special had happened. In our world, anyway."

● *Wagner in 1914. The bats in those days had almost the same circumference from top to bottom.*
National Baseball Library, Cooperstown, NY.

RABBIT MARANVILLE

Impish. You don't often hear that word applied to a major league ballplayer, especially one with 23 years of service. The assumption is that with such longevity at the top, eventually a ballplayer is instilled with a certain measure of decorum. But James Walter Vincent Maranville, known within and without the sporting universe as "Rabbit," maintained, to the end, his impishness and a distance from decorum. While Maranville said "I never lost my dignity," some people might say Rabbit's dignity was uniquely tailored to him.

Maranville spent his sixty-two years of life squeezing out every ounce of talent (which was considerable) and joy (even more considerable) from his 5' 5'' 155-pound frame. He was a wit, a prankster of uninhibited spontaneity, a skilled boxer, wrestler, golfer, fisherman, footballer, basketballer, and, most conspicuously, a highly skilled big-league shortstop for two decades. The pilot light on a "miracle" team, he ended up in the Hall of Fame.

How good a shortstop was Maranville? Most of the eyewitnesses who saw Rabbit in his heyday are no longer here to tell the tale, but the testimony of Hall of Fame outfielder Max Carey, who played both with and against Rabbit, is a cogent summation. "He was just a .258 lifetime hitter," Carey said, "but he still made the Hall of Fame. That tells you how good he was with that glove."

Rabbit's peccadilloes often diverted appreciation of his playing talents. One summer he took road trips accompanied by a pet monkey. His teammates debated which of the two was the better looking (usually the monkey won) and which had the better manners (often declared a tie). Rabbit once swam the Charles River in Boston to avoid making the half-mile walk to the nearest bridge. On another occasion, he dove fully clothed into the fountain outside of the club's St. Louis hotel and emerged soaking wet with a goldfish clenched between his grinning teeth.

Rabbit could be just as entertaining and unpredictable on the field. The crowd loved his "vest-pocket catches," which describes his last-second flick of the glove as he caught a pop fly

at his belt buckle. He was also known to crawl through an umpire's legs and, on occasion, would sit down on baserunners he had just tagged out as they slid into second.

"He could get away with that stuff," said pitcher Jimmy Ring, a Maranville contemporary, "because he was so small nobody would hit him. But nobody ever really got mad at Rabbit. He was a likable SOB."

"When I first heard about him," Joe McCarthy said, "about all the stunts he pulled, I said to myself that for a fellow to do all those crazy things and still keep his job, he had to be a damned good ballplayer. When I got into the league, I saw that I was right. He was full of fun, but he could play ball."

The son of a policeman, Maranville was born November 11, 1891, in Springfield, Massachusetts. Constable Maranville wanted his muscular youngster to become a steamfitter, but the boy had other ideas. After starring in baseball at Springfield High School and on the local sandlots (during which time he fancied himself a catcher), Rabbit had every intention of pursuing a career in professional baseball.

"He never thought of himself as being too short," a boyhood friend recalled. "He used to say that he was just right, that everybody else was too tall."

Rabbit got into pro ball in 1911 with the New Bedford club of the New England League, and there he was converted to shortstop. He was also tagged with his nickname by a fan amused by the new shortstop's agile bounding around the infield. Others said the name derived from a set of pointy ears, but whatever its origin, Maranville welcomed it. "They'd been calling me 'Stumpy' up until then," he said.

John Montgomery Ward, a star nineteenth-century ballplayer and later part-owner of the Boston Braves, scouted Maranville and, in 1912, bought him for the Braves for $2,200. Rabbit finished the 1912 season—his second in professional baseball—with the Braves, beginning a big-league career that would last until 1935.

In 1913, Maranville went to spring training with the Braves, under new manager George

● *Maranville in 1914, the year of the "Miracle."*

Stallings. The club's apparent shortstop was a rookie named Artie Bues, who happened to be the skipper's nephew. Intent upon winning the job, Maranville went to Stallings and said, "Listen, I think I can beat out your nephew. What I want to know is, how many cousins and uncles do you have behind him?" Stallings laughed, marked Rabbit down for spunk and after watching him in spring training decided that talent superseded kinship. Rabbit became Boston's regular shortstop and batted .247 in his rookie year.

It was a year later, in 1914, that Maranville and his team became famous. The Braves, who had finished fifth the year before, seemed ticketed for an even less distinguished wrapup in 1914, moldering in last place as late as July 18. Outside of second baseman Johnny Evers, the team lacked players of star quality. However,

● *George Stallings.*

● *Johnny Evers.*
National Baseball Library, Cooperstown, NY.

they did have three tireless pitchers about to put together prime seasons: Lefty Tyler and right-handers Dick Rudolph and Bill James. These fellows began pitching superbly and winning methodically. At season's end, Rudolph was 27–10, James 26–7, and Tyler 16–14.

Putting on one of the most memorable sustained drives in baseball history, this unaccountable team won 34 of 44, took over first place for keeps on September 8, and kept going, ending the season with a 10½-game bulge over second-place New York and becoming "The Miracle Braves of 1914."

Aside from their three ace pitchers, the chief engineers of Boston's astonishing drive were Evers and Maranville. No one was surprised by the performance of Evers, who had played on four Chicago Cubs pennant winners. The revelation was Maranville. The 22-year-old Rabbit played with "the drive and enthusiasm of a rookie and the poise of a veteran."

Despite a league-high 65 errors (errors were much more plentiful in those years), Maranville put on the kind of display that would keep him in the forefront of league shortstops for years to come. He led in putouts (407) for the first of four consecutive seasons and six overall, and in assists (574), and with 981 chances, he set a record for shortstops, which has since been broken.

"I don't know whether he infected the team or the team infected him," Evers said of Maranville. "But it got to a point where we believed we would win every game and he got to a point where he believed he could make every play. He'd come poaching into my area sometimes. After I'd make the play I'd look up and there he was, standing next to me. 'What the hell do you want?' I'd ask. He'd just mutter and go back to his position. But I knew what it was: he was so keyed up he wanted to take everything."

Miller Huggins, manager of the St. Louis Cardinals that year, said, "There weren't many better clutch hitters than Maranville in 1914." Despite a .246 batting average, Rabbit drove in 72 runs, best on the club.

The Braves continued their "miracle" run in the World Series, upsetting Connie Mack's prohibitively favored Philadelphia Athletics in four straight games. Maranville contributed a .304 average to the cause.

The Braves' success captured the imagination of the country, and because of his carbonated personality, Rabbit was hired to appear on the vaudeville stage that winter. Star ballplayers were frequently booked on the circuit in those years.

Part of Maranville's baseball-oriented act was to re-create his World Series heroics. One night, while demonstrating how he had stolen second base during the Series, he put a bit too much realism into the performance. Running across the stage, he slid so vigorously that he sailed off the stage, dropped into the orchestra pit, and went through a snare drum and broke his foot.

Surviving the perils of the vaudeville stage, Rabbit maintained his status as one of baseball's top defensive shortstops, steadily reducing his error count. In February 1921, he was traded to the Pirates for three players and $15,000. The Pirates believed Rabbit was the man who could come closest to replacing the irreplaceable Wagner, who had retired four years before.

Playing on what in the context of baseball was hallowed ground, Rabbit hit .294 in 1921 and .295 a year later, his top offensive seasons. When the Pirates brought up Glenn Wright in 1924, Maranville moved to second base, where he showed his versatility by leading the position in assists and fielding average. After the 1924 season, he went to Chicago as part of a six-man deal.

● *Maranville with Pittsburgh in 1921.
National Baseball Library, Cooperstown, NY.*

Midway through the 1925 season, Cubs skipper Bill Killefer resigned, and the team decided to replace him with Maranville. Totally ill-suited for managerial responsibilities, Rabbit nevertheless reveled in the job.

After winning his first game (in New York) as skipper, Rabbit and several companions went out to celebrate among New York's speakeasies. Later, with a most exhilarating evening behind them, the celebrants spilled out of a taxi and neglected to tip the driver. Heated dialogue followed, and soon the manager-shortstop of the Chicago Cubs and the hackie were rolling in combat across the sidewalks of New York.

A police contingent appeared on the scene and hauled the two belligerents off to the nearest precinct house. Before a judge the next morning, neither man would testify against the other. When the judge, curious, asked Rabbit why he had failed to tip the driver, Rabbit answered, "It was tradition."

"Tradition?" the judge asked.

"Yes, your Honor. Ballplayers have always been known as cheapskates, and we were simply observing the tradition."

Cubs president William Veeck, Sr., was a man with a sense of humor, and though he could accept a brawling skipper, Veeck could not embrace a skipper who went dancing through a Pullman car one night splashing the occupants with ice water. Veeck felt that managers required more dignity than shortstops, and Maranville was fired. Soon after, Rabbit, as shortstop, was wearing the uniform of the St. Louis Cardinals.

In 1928, the thirty-six-year-old Maranville was at short when the Cardinals edged out the Giants in a bruising pennant race.

"We couldn't have won it without the little bastard," second baseman Frankie Frisch said affectionately. "Playing with him every day made me realize just how good he was, even at his age."

Age, however, seemed irrelevant to Rabbit. As late as 1933, he was playing a full season, at second base, with his original employers, the Boston Braves. He had rejoined the team in 1929.

Rabbit was looking forward to another season in the spring of 1934 when he broke his leg trying to steal home in an exhibition game. A reporter asked the forty-two-year-old Maranville why he was trying to steal home in an exhibition game, and Rabbit replied, "A young fellow has to make a good impression in spring training."

Maranville missed the entire 1934 season, but returned for 23 games in 1935 and reluctantly called it a career. He spent the next half dozen years managing in the minor leagues.

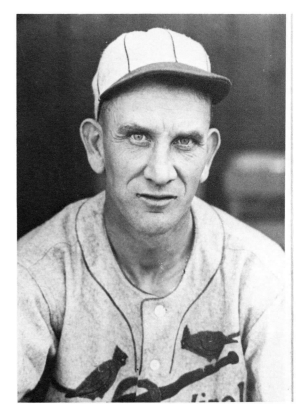

● *Maranville in 1928, the year he helped the Cardinals to the pennant.*
National Baseball Library, Cooperstown, NY.

While managing the Eastern League's Albany club, he could still get into a handful of games playing second base until as late as 1939.

At his retirement, Maranville held the major-league record for most games played by a shortstop, with 2,154. He is now fifth on the all-time list. His 407 assists in 1914 remain the National League record, as does his career mark of 7,338 assists. His major-league records include most times leading in putouts (6) and most lifetime putouts (5,133). And as far as is known, no other big-league shortstop ever sat down on a runner after tagging him out.

● *Maranville in 1935, his final big league year.*
National Baseball Library, Cooperstown, NY.

Rabbit did it all, the serious and the mischievous, with deftness, elan, and some of the purest joy ever seen on a baseball diamond.

Maranville was duly recognized and honored in 1954, when he was elected to the baseball Hall of Fame. Among nineteenth-century shortstops, only Honus Wagner and Joe Tinker beat the little man from Springfield to baseball's most celebrated wall of plaques. Sadly, Rabbit wasn't there to spice the occasion with his wit and charm; he had died a few weeks before his election, on January 5, 1954.

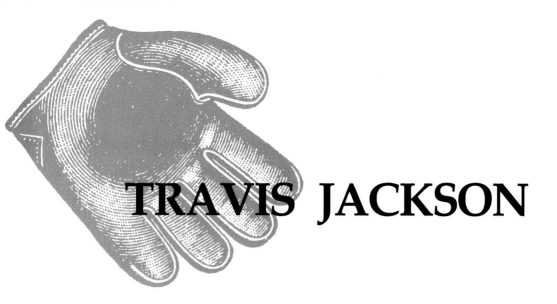

TRAVIS JACKSON

The late Red Smith, America's premier sportswriter, once said Travis Jackson "was the greatest shortstop ever to play in New York." While Smith appreciated the talents of such men as Dave Bancroft, Frank Crosetti, Billy Jurges, Phil Rizzuto, and Pee Wee Reese, he maintained that in all-around ability none could match Travis Jackson.

Burleigh Grimes, Hall of Fame pitcher and teammate of Jackson's for a brief time, said that Jackson's many dimensions could not be matched, even though Pittsburgh's Glenn Wright was outstanding and the Cubs' Charlie Hollocher might have been the most gifted shortstop of the time, but illness cut short Hollocher's career, leaving his ranking inconclusive.

"Wright was famous for his arm," Grimes said, "but Jackson's was just as strong and he could cover more ground, and he had much surer hands. As hitters they were pretty much equal, though I'd give Jackson the edge in power."

Jackson was born on November 2, 1903, in the small southwestern Arkansas town of Waldo. Baseball was a passion for the youngster growing up in the warm, woodsy Arkansas summers. He played on the camel-back diamonds where all youngsters begin, in high school, on the Waldo town team, and then semi-pro ball in the nearby town of Marvell. There he polished, in rural isolation, the skills that would eventually have him playing for baseball's most famous manager and team, in the country's biggest city.

Jackson's local reputation grew, and soon he was being scouted by the Little Rock club of the Southern Association which signed him late in the 1921 season, several months before his eighteenth birthday.

Jackson played the full year with Little Rock in 1922, batted .280, and made the somnolent afternoons of summertime Arkansas crackle with the strength of his throwing arm.

The youngster's arm was strong but erratic—he made a woeful 73 errors, most of them on errant throws. But his manager, Kid Elberfeld, himself a former big league shortstop, told Jackson not to

worry and to keep firing his pegs, that accuracy would soon assert itself, which of course it did.

Elberfeld recommended Jackson to the New York Giants, whose manager John McGraw accepted Elberfeld's evaluation and bought the youngster for baseball's most celebrated and dominant team at that time. (The Yankees, led by Babe Ruth, were just beginning to build their dynasty.)

Jackson was a utility player in 1923, and then took over as the Giants' regular shortstop in 1924. McGraw had been so impressed by the twenty-year-old Jackson that after the 1923 season, the Giants traded their regular shortstop Dave Bancroft to the Boston Braves.

"That was kind of rough on me," Jackson recalled years later. "Not only was I being asked to replace the regular shortstop on a pennant-winning team, but Dave was a very popular player with the Polo Grounds fans." The Giants, with Bancroft at short, had actually taken three straight pennants.

"Jackson did extremely well under difficult conditions," teammate Freddie Lindstrom said. "Bancroft was a talented and well-liked player. But Travis soon won them over. He had a style of play that wasn't flashy but it was very solid. He carried himself with a professionalism on the field that won respect."

Jackson batted .302 in his first full season and helped the Giants to a fourth straight pennant, a team achievement unprecedented in big-league baseball at that time.

"It wasn't easy for him," Grimes said, "because he was breaking in on one of the most powerful teams in history. You might think it's easier to play on a good team than a poor one, but that's not true, and it especially wasn't true of the Giants in those days. Practically the whole team was Hall of Fame. When Jackson joined them they had George Kelly and Bill Terry sharing first base, Frankie Frisch at second, Fred Lindstrom at third, and Ross Youngs and Hack Wilson in the outfield, not to mention McGraw. That's Hall of Fame, all of them. Then a few years later they added Rogers Hornsby, Edd Roush,

● *Jackson unloading during spring training in 1925.*

Mel Ott, and some others. That was a hell of an aggregation, not easy to keep up with, especially for a youngster. But Jackson soon proved that he belonged right there with them."

One afternoon in the summer of 1927, Jackson gave a quiet demonstration of leadership that Lindstrom was to recall years later.

"We had traded Frisch for Hornsby," Lindstrom said. "Now Rogers Hornsby may well have been the greatest hitter that ever lived, but without a bat in his hands he was nothing special. He was, in fact, not very likable, nor did he try to make himself likable. He was outspoken and brutally frank. He would answer any question right to the point and beyond. The man was absolutely without tact. One day one of the writers asked him about a kid pitcher we were carrying who wasn't doing very well. 'He has no business being in the major leagues,' Rogers said. Well, that's not the kind of thing you say to a newspaperman about a teammate.

● *Rogers Hornsby: ". . . outspoken and brutally frank."*
National Baseball Library, Cooperstown, NY.

"The next day Rogers showed up and was greeted by an ice-cold clubhouse. That didn't bother him, of course. He probably didn't even know what it was all about, if he even noticed it. He was getting into his uniform when all of a sudden, from across the clubhouse, Jackson said quietly, 'Hey, Mr. Hornsby. That wasn't a very nice thing you said in the paper yesterday.' That was all. But it made Hornsby take notice of the chill in the clubhouse. And then for the next few days everybody picked up on it and whenever anybody had to address him, it was 'Mr. Hornsby.' It was a sort of ostracism and it wasn't lost on him. He tempered his remarks after that. Jackson had struck just the right note."

Jackson was central to the strong Giants teams of the late 1920s and 1930s. He was a strong-armed, sure-fielding shortstop who "hit more than enough": six times over .300, six times in double figures in home runs, three times with 90 or more runs batted in.

Like so many other National Leaguers, Jackson had his best offensive outing in the hit-happy 1930 season, when the league unloaded on a particularly lively ball. Jackson's contribution to the bruising of the pitchers was a .339 batting average, his personal high. With first baseman Terry batting .401, second baseman Hughie Critz .265, and third baseman Lindstrom .379, the Giants infield had a composite batting average of .346, highest of any infield in baseball history.

By the time the Giants began winning pennants again, in the 1930's, Jackson's playing time was being severely reduced by knee injuries. In the pennant year of 1933, he played in only 53 games, and when the Giants won the pennant again in 1936, his last full season, Jackson was playing third base. The aching knees that had limited his mobility and made him a third baseman after a dozen outstanding years at shortstop, finally forced him into premature retirement after the 1936 season. He was just thirty-three years old.

In an interview late in his life, Jackson, who had spent his entire fifteen-year big-league career with the New York Giants, lamented the destruction of his old home field, the Polo Grounds.

"My whole career was spent there," he said, "and whenever I think of myself as a ballplayer, it's always in the Polo Grounds. Whenever I think of McGraw or Terry or Ott or Hubbell, I see them in the Polo Grounds. And now it's gone, knocked down and built upon. It's like a part of your life's been wiped out."

Jackson's career, however, was to be permanently honored. In 1982, he was elected to the Hall of Fame at Cooperstown, New York. Five years later, on July 17, 1987, the eighty-three-year-old former shortstop died at Waldo, Arkansas, where he had been born, and from where he had gone to stardom.

● *Four members of the New York Giants touring a Hollywood studio in early 1932. Left to right: Freddie Lindstrom, coach Dave Bancroft, Travis Jackson and Bill Terry. The heavy hitter in front is Harpo Marx.*
National Baseball Library, Cooperstown, NY.

● *Jackson in 1936.*
National Baseball Library, Cooperstown, NY.

Pittsburgh Pirate rookie Joe Cronin in 1926.

National Baseball Library, Cooperstown, NY.

JOE CRONIN

Baseball is a game that often wraps its philosophy in tidy axioms, such as "I'd rather be lucky than good." Well, Joe Cronin was both, as befits a man whose career was a constant upward spiral from player to manager to general manager to league president, a unique career embossed with the game's ultimate tap on the shoulder—election to the Hall of Fame.

Cronin's natural assets included a well-swung bat, a strong arm, a gritty knack for self-improvement, and a flair for leadership. By his incalculable luck, he was often in the right place at the right time, marrying his boss's niece, and later working for another boss who showed him absolute loyalty and boundless respect.

Cronin was born on October 12, 1906, in San Francisco, six months after the city's famous earthquake. The Cronin household had been wiped out in the quake, except for a single rocking chair.

In his later years, as American League president, Joe presented a generously rounded silhouette, but as a youngster he was tall and wiry. A gifted athlete, he excelled at basketball, soccer, and baseball while in high school, and even won a city-wide junior championship at tennis when he was just fourteen. Offered an athletic scholarship at San Francisco's St. Mary's College, he turned it down to go to work to help his hard-pressed family.

Joe took a job as a playground instructor and supplemented his earnings by playing semi-pro ball around the Bay area. He soon gained a reputation for his infield work and his line-drive bat. In 1925, a Pittsburgh Pirate scout spotted him and signed him to a contract. Cronin's debut took place in Johnstown, Pennsylvania, an outpost in the Mid-Atlantic League. Nearly a full continent away from his California home, Cronin began a career that lasted the next half century.

Joe batted .313 for Johnstown, and the Pirates, impressed with the young man's stickwork, brought him to the big leagues in 1926. Unfortunately for Cronin, the Pirates already had a fixture at shortstop— Glenn Wright, and another at third base—Pie Traynor.

With no openings for the slim, lantern-jawed youngster, Cronin was farmed out in mid-season to New Haven in the Eastern League. There he played shortstop and batted .320 in 66 games.

Cronin spent the entire 1927 season with the Pirates; but for Joe it was a prolonged exercise in inactivity. Playing in only 12 games, Cronin sat in the dugout shade and watched his teammates win the National League pennant. Continuing his role of uniformed spectator, he watched as the Yankees flattened the Pirates in four straight in the World Series.

Seeing no future for him in Pittsburgh, the Pirates sold Cronin's contract to Kansas City of the American Association. In mid-season 1928, he was batting just .245 and was about to be sent down to a lower minor league when he enjoyed a stroke of the Cronin luck. A scout for the Washington Senators saw him and recommended him to Clark Griffith, who grudgingly dented his zealously guarded vaults to shell out $7,500 for Joe's contract. So instead of making a career descent, Cronin jumped to the major leagues. In 63 games at shortstop for Washington, he batted .242 and fielded tolerably well.

"At the time," Griffith said, "it wasn't apparent what a great player he was going to become, but he did have a mature, self-assured quality about him that you had to like."

Cronin joined a fairly strong Washington club, with a lineup featuring first baseman Joe Judge, manager and second baseman Bucky Harris, and outfielders Sam Rice, Goose Goslin, and Sammy West. Harris had been managing the club since 1924, when he was a twenty-seven-year-old "Boy Manager" who went on to win pennants in his first two years.

In 1929, Cronin's first full year with the Senators, the recently retired Walter Johnson took over as manager. Walter liked Cronin's style and installed the young man at shortstop. "He's as serious as a banker out there," the old pitcher said. Joe responded with a .281 batting average, but committed a bushel basket full of errors—62.

● *Walter Johnson (left) and Clark Griffith.*
National Baseball Library, Cooperstown, NY.

Cronin went home to San Francisco that winter with two goals in mind for the 1930 season: raise his batting average and reduce his error total. When he showed up for spring training in 1930, he seemed transformed.

"I don't know what the heck he did over the winter," third baseman Ossie Bluege said, "but he had put on about fifteen pounds and was so much bigger and stronger." What Joe had done was to run five miles every day and work in a forest north of San Francisco cutting down trees.

"You could see as soon as he stepped into the box," Bluege said, "that he was a better hitter, really whacking the ball hard. And through hard work he was making himself a better fielder. Joe was never a Honus Wagner in the field, but he

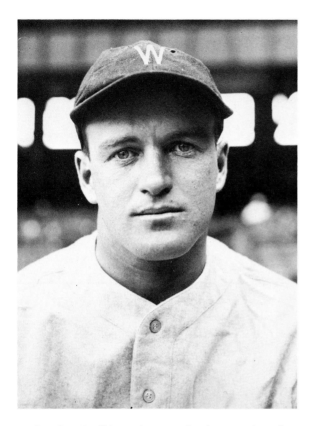

● *Joe Cronin: "As serious as a banker out there."*

made himself into a damned good shortstop through sheer hard work and determination."

The 1930 season put Cronin on the road to stardom. He attained career highs with a .346 batting average, 126 runs batted in, and 203 hits. In addition, he cut his errors to 35 and led league shortstops in putouts and assists.

"In a year or two," Bluege said, "Cronin was the best shortstop in the league, bar none. And he was a dynamic leader on the field. He was a natural leader, as Harris had been. That wasn't lost on the Old Man."

The Old Man was Griffith. After the 1932 season, Griff decided that the gentlemanly Johnson wasn't supplying the leadership the talented Washington team needed and a managerial change was in order. Recalling the suc-

cess he had had with the twenty-seven-year-old Harris in 1924, Griffith hired his twenty-six-year-old shortstop as his new manager.

Driven and goaded by their new skipper—the youngest man on the team—the Senators won the pennant in 1933, finishing seven games ahead of a power-laden New York Yankee club. Though they lost the World Series to the New York Giants, the Senators led their league with a .287 batting average, including Cronin's .309. Joe topped the club with 118 RBIs and the league with 45 doubles. This was his watershed year; already established as the league's top shortstop, Cronin was now, at a baseball-tender age, a successful manager.

Beset by injuries in 1934, the Senators sank to seventh place. For Cronin, a disappointing season was followed by a joyous post-season, for that fall he married Mildred Griffith, the niece of Clark Griffith.

It was said that the tight-fisted Griffith would have sold his mother if the price were right. Well, while what value the Washington owner might have placed upon his mother was never put to the test, he did receive a generous offer for the newest member of his family.

Boston Red Sox owner Tom Yawkey, eager to build his newly acquired club into a winner, wanted Cronin to manage and play shortstop and was willing to part with $250,000 for the privilege. In the Depression-ridden America of 1934, a quarter of a million dollars was a phenomenal amount of money and enough to give a penny counter like Griffith a case of vertigo. Griff accepted the offer, but not before cutting a favorable deal for Cronin, of whom he was genuinely fond.

At Griffith's prodding, Yawkey agreed to give Cronin a five-year contract as player-manager at $50,000 a year. When Griffith broke the news of the transaction to Joe, he was pleased, because aside from the money and the security, Joe had been concerned about how becoming a Griffith family member might affect his relationship with Griffith and with the Washington players.

● *Washington's youthful skipper in 1933.*

● *Cronin (left) and Tom Yawkey in the spring of 1935.*

"Being so close with the owner of the club could have proved to be troublesome," Cronin said later, "and even though my years in Washington had been enjoyable ones, I think it was a good time to make a change."

Throughout his long tenure as manager of the Red Sox, Cronin's generally hard-hitting, weak-pitching teams shared a common problem with the rest of the American League: the New York Yankees, who took seven of eight pennants between 1936 and 1943. Joe's job was never in jeopardy, however, because of the rapport he had established with Yawkey, who always held Cronin in the highest esteem. The relationship, in fact, might have been detrimental to Red Sox fortunes, for Yawkey usually deferred to Cron-

in's evaluations of talent which, according to some people, were not always the keenest.

Cronin continued his solid hitting in Fenway Park, going over .300 four times, driving in over 90 runs six times, and leading the league with 51 doubles in 1938. Though never brilliant in the field, Cronin was considered more than adequate, with a strong arm as his greatest asset. And he did lead league shortstops in putouts and assists, three times each, and in fielding, twice.

As manager of the Red Sox, Cronin was handed some singular personalities, like Bobo Newsom. Garrulous, colorful, and talented, the rubber-armed right-hander pitched for the Red Sox for just a few months in 1937, and the following episode will help explain the brevity: Bobo was on the Boston mound one afternoon

● Red Sox manager—shortstop Joe Cronin.
National Baseball Library, Cooperstown, NY.

● Ted Williams, Cronin's biggest headache and
greatest joy.
National Baseball Library, Cooperstown, NY.

and found himself in a tight spot. Cronin trotted over to the mound to offer some advice, only to have his pitcher squint disdainfully at him and say, "Who's telling Old Bobo how to pitch?"

Cronin also had to contend with outfielder Ben Chapman who, despite a .340 batting average in 1938, did not linger long at Fenway Park. Though a gifted player, Ben once ignored a bunt sign, then proceeded to ground into a double play. When Cronin asked for an explanation, Ben was bluntly direct: "I don't bunt."

Joe received the most resolute individualist of them all in the spring of 1938, when a tall, skinny, good-looking youngster came to camp. Calling the skipper "Sport," Ted Williams amused the veterans with his cockiness and self-confidence.

"His self-confidence wasn't misplaced," Cronin said. "He was the greatest hitter I ever saw."

Williams admired and respected Cronin, calling him "a player's manager."

According to outfielder Doc Cramer, "You had more than just a teammate and a manager when you played for Joe. If a fight broke out on the field, Joe was the first one into it, looking

● Cronin (right) and the man he succeeded as
American League president, Will Harridge, seen
here in the spring of 1947.

out for his players. He'd duke it out with anybody, and I never saw the man who could make
him back up."

Manager Cronin kept shortstop Cronin in
the regular lineup until 1941, when he moved
aside for young Johnny Pesky. The depletion of
big-league rosters during the war years kept Joe
on the active lists as a part-timer and pinch-hitter
until 1945. In 1943, he set a league record by
pinch-hitting five home runs, underlining what
Connie Mack had once said of Joe's propensities
in the clutch: "With a man on third and one out,
I'd rather have Cronin hitting for me than anybody I've ever seen."

Cronin's playing career came to a sudden
end on April 19, 1945, when he broke his leg in

a game against the Yankees. Thereafter he was
strictly a bench manager. In 1946, his 12th year
as Red Sox manager, he finally brought home
the pennant that he and Yawkey had been
waiting for. (The Sox lost an exciting seven-game
World Series to the St. Louis Cardinals.)

After a final year in the dugout in 1947,
Cronin was elevated to the executive suite as
vice-president, treasurer, and general manager
of the Red Sox. In 1956, he was elected to the
Hall of Fame, and three years later, he became
president of the American League, a post he oc-
cupied until 1973.

Cronin died on September 7, 1984, a few
weeks before his seventy-eighth birthday.

Luke Appling.

LUKE APPLING

Luke Appling played in the major leagues for twenty years. He is a Hall of Fame shortstop, two-time batting champion, lifetime .300 hitter. Nevertheless, what many opposing pitchers remember most vividly about the affable, easy-going Appling was his uncanny ability to nick foul balls virtually at will. If this seems at best a marginal talent, perhaps one ought to listen to the testimony of one of the pitchers who was victimized by the skill that Appling sometimes employed mischievously and at other times to gain tactical advantage.

"It was my first full year in the league and I was pitching against the White Sox on a blazing hot day in Chicago, said Vic Raschi, ace New York Yankee right-hander during the late 1940s and early 1950s. "It was the seventh inning and we were leading by a run. I was out on the mound, sweating like a pig, trying to conserve my strength. I glanced over at the White Sox dugout for a moment and there was Appling, sitting there with his fingertips on his chin, watching me like a hawk. Two batters later, he's at the plate. I got two strikes on him and then he began fouling them off. They told me later that he fouled off about fourteen or fifteen

pitches, every one of which I threw as hard as I could. I finally got him out, but he had achieved his purpose—wearing me out. The next inning I had nothing and they hit me hard. Thanks to Appling. There wasn't another hitter who could do what he did."

It was Appling's intention that day to wear out the young Raschi. But on other occasions, according to Detroit right-hander Dizzy Trout, "He stands there and fouls off ten or twelve of your best pitches, waiting for one that he feels he can hit safely. How does that make you feel out there on the mound? I'll tell you how it makes you feel—like a damned batting practice pitcher. The more he fouls off, the madder you get, and the madder you get, the more apt you are to make a mistake."

Appling's magical way with a baseball bat produced 2,749 career hits and a long string of .300-plus batting averages, including a monumental.388 mark in 1936, the highest ever recorded by a major-league shortstop.

This amiable, unpretentious manufacturer of line drives was born Lucius Benjamin Appling, on April 2, 1909, in High Point, North Carolina. When he was a boy, his family moved to Atlanta. It was in this Georgia city that he began cultivating his athletic skills, first as a shortstop at Atlanta's Fulton High School and then, later, at Oglethorpe University.

In college, he played basketball and was quarterback for the football team, but it was his work on the diamond that attracted the scouts. In 1930 the local boy signed with the local team—the Atlanta Crackers, an independently owned club in the Southern Association.

The rookie shortstop batted .326 and, near the end of the season, was sold to the Chicago White Sox, whom he joined in September. With the White Sox, Luke got into six games and batted .308, two points under the career average he would leave behind 20 years later.

When he heard he had been sold to Chicago, Appling initially believed he was headed for the Cubs. This delighted him because the Cubs were at that time one of the power teams in baseball. Though the Cubs had put in a bid for Luke, the White Sox topped the offer, and so he was off to Comiskey Park.

Like teammate Ted Lyons, the club's outstanding pitcher, Appling was doomed to a long career in the gloomy regions of the American League standings. The White Sox finished in the second division in 15 of Luke's 20 seasons and never placed higher than third.

Appling was an unpolished performer in his early big league days, particularly in the field. In 96 games in 1931, he made 43 errors. But Luke got a break in 1933, when the White Sox obtained veteran third baseman Jimmy Dykes from the Philadelphia Athletics. Dykes, who would soon begin a 13-year tenure as White Sox manager, enrolled Luke for a course of personal tutelage. According to Appling, Dykes "did more for me than any other man in baseball." Under Dykes's shrewd coaching, instruction, and good-natured needling, Appling gradually became a much improved fielder. Though Luke would

● *Yankee right-hander Vic Raschi: "There wasn't another hitter who could do what Appling did." National Baseball Library, Cooperstown, NY.*

continue to make his share of errors—leading the league five times in this basement statistic, he also led seven times in assists.

Appling came to be considered a good, though never great, defensive player. However, Dykes insisted that Luke could cover as much ground as any shortstop he had ever seen. But the question of Appling's fielding was probably answered definitively by Lyons, who said, "A man doesn't play shortstop in the big leagues for twenty years unless he can handle the position

● *Luke Appling: ". . . affable, easy-going."*

damned well." By his retirement in 1950, Appling had played the position for a record 2,218 games.

After batting .232 and .274 in his first two seasons, Appling began his long string of .300 batting averages. In 15 of his next 16 full seasons, he surpassed .300. Swinging from an open stance, lining most of his hits into right and right-center, Luke became one of baseball's most proficient and consistent hitters.

"He was the most relaxed man at the plate I ever saw," Lyons said. "It was an off-shoot of his personality. Luke was always amiable, always smiling. He went up to the plate like that, perfectly at his ease, perfectly confident."

In 1936, Luke rang up his landmark season of .388, becoming the first American League shortstop and the only White Sox player, to win a batting championship. In Dykes's words, Luke was "deadly accurate" all year. "No matter how

they pitched him and no matter how they played him—bang!—a line drive base hit to right-center. You could have set your clock by him that year."

Appling delivered 204 hits in 1936, of which 160 were singles. But he drove in a career-high 128 runs, despite hitting just six home runs. Yankee pitcher Red Ruffing grumbled that he could explain Luke's success: "He always gets a good pitch to hit." Pressed further, Ruffing said, "He just stands there fouling them off until he gets one he can drive. I would rather pitch to Jimmie Foxx or Hank Greenberg or anybody else except Appling. The nicest guy in the world, but when he's up at the plate you want to drill him."

Along with his base hits and his foul balls, Appling was also known as a "groaner." A man of many sad complaints about his physical condition, Appling's frequent lamentations about ailments real or imaginary earned him the nickname "Old aches and pains."

"He'd come to me before a game," Dykes said, "and tell me his shoulder or his ankle was killing him, and I'd pat him on the back and tell him to go out and do the best he could, and out he'd go and rap two or three hits. One time I asked him how he was and he said he felt like he was dying. I told him if he was dying then he might as well do it out at shortstop, that that would be most appropriate. I think he got three hits that day."

Luke had this explanation for his legendary ailments:

"I used to room with the team trainer. He had to be at the park early, and I usually went along with him and took a snooze on the rubbing table while he got his stuff ready. If the other players came in and I was sleeping, he would tell them not to bother me because he was giving me special treatment for a sore back or a pulled muscle. I guess that's where everybody got the idea that I was always ailing. Actually, I was a fairly healthy guy." In fact during 14 of his 15 full seasons in the big leagues, Luke played in 139 or more games.

● *White Sox manager Jimmy Dykes (right)*
explaining the situation to umpire Cal Hubbard.

During spring training in 1938, Appling broke his leg sliding into a base. Because of his reputation for "groaning," Luke said, "They wouldn't believe I was really hurt until two doctors looked me over and said my leg was broken."

Appling batted .348 in 1940, which he later said was a better year than his .388 showing because he "hit the ball better and more consis- tently that season than any other." He was in the batting race all summer with Joe DiMaggio, losing out on the season's final day to Joe's .352.

After dropping to an uncharacteristic .262 in 1942, Appling came back a year later to take his second batting title with a .328 mark. That winter he entered the Army, at which time his wife remarked, "The war can't last very long now. Why, except for baseball, Luke's never held a job more than two weeks in his life."

● *Appling demonstrating just how easy it was to play shortstop.*

● *Appling in 1950, his last year as an active player.*

However, despite his previous employment history, Luke held this job for about 20 months. After he was discharged in September 1945, he headed straight for Chicago, reclaimed his old post at shortstop, and demonstrated his deft touch at the plate by batting .362 in 18 games.

Appling kept ringing up .300 averages, hitting line drives, nicking foul balls, and letting everyone know about his aches and pains. In 1949, at the age of forty-two, he played 141 games at shortstop and batted .301. A year later, he got into just 50 games, batted a telltale .234, and retired from active play. Thereafter he worked as a minor league manager, a big-league coach (his specialty was batting), and a scout.

In 1964, Appling was elected to the Hall of Fame. On the day of his election, a reporter asked him how he felt upon achieving a ballplayer's most cherished honor.

Uncharacteristically, Luke replied, "Great. I feel just great." When Jimmy Dykes heard of the comment, Luke's old skipper said, "I guess that's all he needed to make him feel better—just a little thing like making the Hall of Fame."

Luke Appling died on January 3, 1991.

The quiet man, Arky Vaughan.

ARKY VAUGHAN

Decade after decade Arky Vaughan remained one of the most inexplicable omissions from baseball's Hall of Fame. One old-time baseball writer, who maintained a steady campaign for Vaughan's election, said, "Part of the problem is Vaughan himself. The guy was always so damned reticent and modest about himself. No temperament, no ego, no vanity. Just a history of superlative achievements." It was as though Vaughan had passed across the grass of baseball America like a shadow, leaving behind neither stir nor footprint.

Perhaps Vaughan's archetypical day in baseball was the occasion of the 1941 All-Star Game. Not known for his long-ball bat, Arky had banged out a pair of home runs in the game, supplying the power that sent the National League winging into the bottom of the ninth inning with a 5–4 lead. But just as Vaughan was about to be hailed as the hero of the game, Ted Williams erupted with a stunning two-out, three-run home run that gave the American League the victory and Williams the headlines.

"Everybody in the press box," one writer recalled, "quickly erased 'Vaughan' from their leads and substituted 'Williams.' "

But Arky's contemporaries knew how good he was. Honus Wagner, coaching Vaughan's Pittsburgh Pirates in the 1930s, said of the young shortstop, "I get a great kick out of watching that kid. He hasn't a batting weakness. One of the sweetest hitters I ever saw. And fast! They don't make 'em any faster. He's improved a lot as a fielder, too."

Vaughan's development as a fielder may or may not have been attributable to Wagner. When Arky reported to the Pirates' camp as a rookie, he was turned over to Honus. The bulky, bow-legged paragon of all shortstops asked the youngster what his problems were at the position.

"Slow rollers, mainly," Vaughan said.

"They're easy," Wagner said. "All you have to do is run in fast, pick up the ball, and get it to first base ahead of the runner."

"Well, I know that," Vaughan said. "But can you give me some pointers?"

Wagner frowned for a moment, then said,

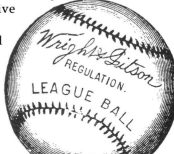

● *Paul Waner.*

● *Arky Vaughan: ". . . clean smashes over the infield."*

"You don't need any pointers. I just told you how to do it."

Vaughan played America's game with a seamless expertise: steady in the field, a blur on the basepaths, and a batter whose hits were, in the words of one writer, "usually straight on the nose, long, clean, smashing hits."

Teammate Paul Waner, one of the most skilled of all big-league hitters, reflected on Arky's sizzling line drives: "Vaughan is one of the fastest men in baseball. He can get down to first like a flash. Yet, I doubt if he made six hits all season long by foot work alone. Almost all of his hits were clean smashes over the infield or to the distant outfield. Fast men get many flukey hits, usually Vaughan doesn't."

The future shortstop was born at Clifty, Arkansas, as Joseph Floyd Vaughan, on March 9, 1912. When he was a child, the family moved to a ranch near Fullerton, California, where the youngster cultivated a lifelong delight in fishing and hunting, as well as his skills at baseball. When his friends found out he had been born in Arkansas, they gave him the nickname "Arky" which was to adhere so completely that, as Vaughan once remarked, "Most people have no idea what my given name really is."

A New York Yankee scout was interested in Vaughan, but before he could act, Art Grigg—owner of the Pirate farm club in Wichita, Kansas, of the Western Association—signed Arky, and in 1931 the nineteen-year-old shortstop entered pro ball. After a .338 season at Wichita, Vaughan was brought to the Pirates' spring camp in 1932 for a look.

"Never said a word," Pirates outfielder Lloyd Waner remembered. "He was a sharp kid, paid attention to everything, but never said a word. But you noticed him: he could field, could hit, and ran like a rabbit. He was supposed to go out for another year of seasoning, but then our regular shortstop Tommy Thevenow got hurt and the club decided to play the kid. It turned out to be a pretty good idea."

Vaughan got into the lineup, started hitting, and never stopped. He batted .300 or better in each of his first ten big-league seasons, and soared to a league-leading .385 average in 1935 (a mark which no National League hitter has come close to since). That same year, Vaughan also attained personal peaks with 19 home runs and 99 runs batted in.

Among his accomplishments, Vaughan led the league for three years in triples, three in runs scored, one in slugging, one in stolen bases, and three consecutive years in bases on balls. Afield, he led league shortstops three times each in put-outs and assists.

Vaughan, however, was a man whose still waters contained an occasional riptide. One day, while attempting to complete a double play, Arky's relay to first accidentally made thudding contact with the head of the baserunner, Dick Bartell. Bartell, a fiery character, did not think the errant throw was accidental and said so to the press, adding the warning that he would get even. Vaughan read the story and said nothing.

When their two ball clubs met next, Vaughan crossed the field toward Bartell during batting practice. After handing Bartell a ragged press clipping of the story, Vaughan asked if Bartell had been accurately quoted. Bartell said that he had, and Vaughan suggested the question be settled right then and there. Bartell considered the offer and then declined.

Probably the only recorded story of Arky's temper flaring was an incident in 1943, when he was with the Brooklyn Dodgers. Arky had been traded for four players after the end of the 1941 season (a trade which broke many a heart in Pittsburgh). Dodger skipper Leo Durocher had given an interview to one of the team's writers in which, in the eyes of Vaughan and many of the other Dodgers, Leo had been unfairly critical of one of the team's players. An irate Vaughan walked into Leo's office, threw his uniform across the skipper's desk, and made an indelicate suggestion as to what Leo might do with it.

Though Vaughan threatened to quit, the episode was smoothed over, and Arky finished out the season. When the season ended, however, he returned to his ranch in Mendicino, California, and announced his retirement. He was thirty-two years old.

Four years later the Dodgers talked him out of retirement, and in 1947 he returned as a part-time player. Despite his years away, Arky proved once more that, to paraphrase Gertrude Stein, a hitter was a hitter was a hitter. In 64 games he batted .325 and helped the Dodgers to the pennant, giving the veteran the long-awaited opportunity to play in a World Series.

Vaughan played another year for the Dodgers, then put in some time with San Francisco of the Pacific Coast League, and finally folded up his glove for keeps.

On the afternoon of August 30, 1952, Vaughan and a friend slid their rowboat into the cold waters of a lake near Eagleville, California, for a day's fishing. When they were out in the middle of the lake, the boat somehow capsized and neither Vaughan nor his companion were able to make it back to shore. Arky was just forty years old.

For a long time it seemed as if Arky had taken with him all of his baseball accomplishments. He had become one of the game's forgotten men. But then, in 1985, thirty-seven years after he had played his last big league game, the Hall of Fame electors finally corrected the injustice and formally elected Vaughan to the hierarchy to which he had always belonged.

● *Brooklyn's 1942 infield poses at the team's Havana, Cuba spring training camp. Left to right, Arky Vaughan, Dolf Camilli, Billy Herman, and Pee Wee Reese. With Reese a fixture at short, Vaughan played third for the Dodgers.*

● *Vaughan in 1942.*

• • •

Lou Boudreau in 1939.

National Baseball Library, Cooperstown, NY.

LOU BOUDREAU

Within the most formidable athletes, there is a special talent that enables them to elevate a sport above the status of a mere game and create something symbolic of a nobler spirit. This unique gift is the ability to perform transcendently under pressure, to shape the yardstick by which future heroes will be measured.

Lou Boudreau's performance on the afternoon of October 4, 1948, has been called "memorable," "scintillating," and "inspiring." It was also perfectly within character, for it was typical of Boudreau's theatrical demonstrations.

The Cleveland Indians and the Boston Red Sox were meeting at Fenway Park in the American League's first-ever playoff to decide the pennant winner, each team having completed the season with identical records of 96–58.

The game was weighted with pressure, as the entire 154-game season was about to be compressed into a single afternoon. For the Indians, it was an opportunity to end what was now a generation-long championship drought—1920 had been the last time the team had won a pennant. The city of Cleveland and its fans were primed for a victory, a then all-time attendance record of 2,620,627 having been set.

For Cleveland's manager-shortstop Lou Boudreau, who at the age of thirty was already completing his seventh year as manager, it was the most sublime challenge of his athletic career, and he went at it ravenously. In the top of the first inning, he got his team off to a 1–0 lead by hitting a home run. In the fourth inning, he began a three-run rally with a single. In the fifth inning, he hit another home run. Later he added another single, giving him a 4-for-4 day, with two runs batted in and three scored. In addition he flawlessly handled eight chances in the field.

The final score was 8–3, Cleveland, with Boudreau turning in one of the most exemplary displays of under-the-gun splendor in baseball history.

The future "Boy Manager" of the Cleveland Indians was born on July 17, 1917, at Harvey, Illinois, about 20 miles outside of Chicago.

Gravitating naturally to leadership, Boudreau at age thirteen was the coach of his grammar school basketball team. He went on to Thornton

● *Celebrating Cleveland's pennant-winning victory over Boston in 1948 are (left to right) winning pitcher Gene Bearden, Boudreau, and third baseman Ken Keltner.*
National Baseball Library, Cooperstown, NY.

Township High School, where he was a standout in baseball and basketball, in which he helped the school to a state championship. He made the All-Illinois scholastic team three years in a row, something no other boy had ever achieved.

In his early teenage years, Lou determined he was a catcher, but his father, Louis, Sr., a locally well-known semi-pro third baseman, suggested the boy switch to the infield, which he did.

Boudreau's exploits at high school athletics earned him a scholarship to the University of Illinois at Champaign, a scholarship he subsidized by working in his fraternity house kitchen. Just as he was plunging into higher education, the Cleveland Indians came around and offered him a minor league contract. There were no large bonuses offered to entice a youngster in those days, so Boudreau decided to stay on at Champaign and pursue his education.

The Indians, however, would not be put off. Upon receiving Lou's promise to sign with them when he was ready to enter professional ball, the club agreed to pay the Boudreau family $100 a month as long as he remained an undergraduate. Though meager by later standards, the money was enough to help the Boudreau household through the years of the Depression.

At Illinois, Boudreau made a national name for himself as a basketball player. He was just beginning his junior year when word of the Cleveland payments reached the newspaper. The controversy that ensued raised the question of professionalism and placed Boudreau's college eligibility in doubt. The outcome of the controversy was that Boudreau was suspended from college competition for a year but could be reinstated in his senior year if he severed his relationship with the Indians.

Boudreau decided to finish his junior year and then enter professional baseball. Eventually he completed his senior year and got his degree in Physical Education from Illinois in February 1940.

● *Ray Mack (left) and Boudreau.*
National Baseball Library, Cooperstown, NY.

So in 1938, twenty-year-old Lou Boudreau signed with the Indians and was sent to the Cedar Rapids, Iowa, club in the Three-Eye League. Breaking in as a third baseman, he batted .290. The following spring he was promoted to the Indians' Buffalo club in the International League and switched to shortstop. After 115 games he was batting .331 and, along with second-base partner Ray Mack, was fielding like a demon.

On August 1, the Boudreau-Mack tandem was brought up to Cleveland and immediately became one of the league's dazzling double-play combinations. In 53 games, Boudreau batted .258. His Hall of Fame career was underway.

The Indians and their fans knew almost from the beginning that they had something special in their darkly handsome, personable, intelligent young shortstop. At first it was the rookie's fielding that caused the greatest excitement. He was known for his "lightning reflexes, startlingly fast break, sure hands." One Cleveland sportswriter said, "When the ball is hit on the ground where Boudreau can reach it, the batter is out. A Boudreau error is greeted with a gasp of shocked disbelief."

"He was a marvelous fielder," Yankee manager Joe McCarthy said. "But where he particularly excelled was in making the big play, with runners in scoring position or the game in the balance. They say that DiMaggio was the greatest clutch hitter. Well, maybe Boudreau was the greatest clutch fielder."

Boudreau played on chronically painful ankles. His right one had been broken three times, and both were afflicted with arthritic deposits. Consequently, he lacked outstanding running speed; nevertheless, he was extremely quick at breaking in either direction to snare ground balls.

But Boudreau didn't just make plays in the clutch, he made them all the time. In his first five years, he led American League shortstops in fielding. In 1945 he was in only 97 games because of a fractured ankle and thus was not qualified to lead. But for the next three years, he led in fielding again. His eight fielding titles tie him with Everett Scott and Luis Aparicio for the major-league record for shortstops.

In 1940, his first full season in the big leagues, Boudreau batted .295, which would be his lifetime average when he retired in 1952. He was a line-drive hitter, three times leading the league in doubles (each time with 45), and four times a .300 hitter, winning the batting crown in 1944 with a .327 average.

Writing in *Sport Magazine* in 1948, Ed Fitzgerald described Boudreau at the plate:

His left foot is forward, his weight anchored on his right. His rear end seems to jut halfway to the third-base side dugout, and his chin is buried in the sleeve of his left arm, which is held out ramrod-straight from his shoulder. His right arm is bent easily, ready to supply the power behind his swing. His eyes are glued to the pitcher. . . . You know he's out to get a hit, not a walk. He's absolutely motionless from the time the pitcher goes into his windup. He appears to be stalking his opponent, baiting him, lying in wait for him, ready to pounce. . . .

The Boudreau swing, Fitzgerald went on, was not graceful like DiMaggio or Williams, but was more of "a sudden lash, stunningly swift in its execution."

This is a portrait of an intensely focused athlete. This is the other side of a man described by Cleveland's 1941 manager Roger Peckinpaugh as a "personality kid—it just oozed out of him. Some of the guys felt that his enthusiasm was maybe a bit too college-bred, but it was genuine. Everything about Lou was genuine. He was one hell of a competitor."

Bob Feller, Cleveland's ace of aces, said of Boudreau, "He was a rah-rah guy. But he bristled with confidence and he could play."

It was this confidence that led Boudreau to file an astonishing job application after the 1941 season. Peckinpaugh had been moved up to the general manager's job, and the Indians were looking for a new manager. The twenty-four-year-old Boudreau, who had just completed his second full big-league season, said to himself,

● *Boudreau (left) with his ace of aces, Bob Feller.*

"Why not you?" Unable to find any good reasons why not, he contacted club president Alva Bradley and proposed himself for the job. Bradley thought it over, discussed it with the club's directors, and on November 25, 1941, announced Boudreau's appointment. Lou answered the inevitable questions about playing shortstop and managing by saying, "I can handle it."

He handled it well enough for the next six years, finishing between third and sixth places, and although his clubs were never contenders, Boudreau's popularity in Cleveland remained extremely high.

His most memorable managerial accomplishment during these years was his innovative "Williams Shift," which he devised in July 1946 to alleviate some of the devastation wreaked upon his team by Boston's great slugger. Boudreau loaded the right side of the infield with three infielders and swung his outfield drastically to the right, hoping to intercept Ted's rifle shots and banking on Ted's stubborn pride and determination to try and hit through the Shift instead of to left field. While Williams conceded that the maneuver (soon adapted by other teams) did clip some points from his batting average, he maintained that the damage was mostly "psychological."

After the 1947 season, Bill Veeck, who was running the Indians at the time, dropped some hints that his manager-shortstop was on the trading block. The ensuing uproar from Cleveland fans was of sufficient volume and passion to make the owner change his mind. But, it was now apparent that 1948 was the year Boudreau and his team had to deliver the city's long-deferred pennant.

Like a man on a crusade, Lou Boudreau attacked the 1948 season with an intensity almost impossible to sustain throughout baseball's long season. However, Boudreau, who struck that level on opening day, never relented.

"He didn't play just every game as hard as he could," one writer said, "he played every inning and every pitch with passion and dedication. And when you look at how the season ended, how close it was, you can see he was absolutely right, that his total commitment was essential."

In the season that ended with Boudreau's heroic performance against the Red Sox in the one-game playoff, the Cleveland skipper had batted .355, hit a career-high 18 home runs, drove in 106 runs, had 199 hits, and struck out a remarkably low nine times in 560 official at bats. It was an MVP season for Boudreau, who then led his club to the world championship in six games over the Boston Braves.

The energy Boudreau expended throughout the golden summer of 1948, on both physical and psychic levels, was not replaceable. In fact, he

● *Washington manager Bucky Harris (left) and Boudreau in 1942.*

played only one more full season, and though he played well, it was nowhere near the hell-bent 1948 season.

Boudreau was released by Cleveland in November 1950 and signed by the Red Sox a few days later. He batted .267 in 82 games, and except for a few appearances in 1952, his playing career was over.

Boudreau managed the Red Sox from 1952 to 1954, the Kansas City Athletics from 1955 to 1957, and the Chicago Cubs in 1960, never finishing higher than fourth. He later settled into the more tranquil confines of the broadcasting booth at Wrigley Field.

Cleveland's former "Boy Manager," batting champion, MVP, and record-setting shortstop was voted into baseball's Hall of Fame in 1970.

● *The infield alignment of the "Williams Shift" as devised by Boudreau.*

● *Boudreau with the Boston Red Sox in 1951.*

Pee Wee Reese in 1940. *"He looked like he was twelve years old."*

PEE WEE REESE

For many people it remains one of the purest and most indelible of memories. A lot of stories have and continue to be written about it, and films and still shots preserve the images. But the only way to understand the moment was to have been there, to experience the pinnacle of a half-century's anticipation.

The date was October 4, 1955. The place was New York's Yankee Stadium. The occasion was the seventh game of the World Series, the Brooklyn Dodgers versus the New York Yankees. The Dodgers had never won a World Series; they were winless in seven attempts. But now they were poised at the brink of that long-sought goal.

It was the bottom of the ninth inning, there were two out, the bases empty, the Dodgers led by a 2–0 score. Brooklyn southpaw Johnny Podres, pitching the game of his life, a game that stands in Brooklyn history like some magnificent sculpture, delivered the pitch and Yankee Elston Howard hit it.

The direction of the ball suddenly seemed fitting and appropriate, with an almost honorary quality to it. The ground ball went to shortstop Pee Wee Reese, who fielded it. With a smile breaking across his face, Reese threw the ball to first baseman Gil Hodges, and the Brooklyn Dodgers had one of the most celebrated and bountifully toasted World Series victories in history.

When he picked up that ground ball and brought the dreams of the Brooklyn Dodgers and their fans full circle, Reese was thirty-seven years old and had been playing shortstop for the Dodgers since 1940 (with three years out serving in the United States Navy during World War II). Among Brooklyn's ardently faithful and exuberantly devoted fans, Reese was without peer; under their eyes he had grown from baby-faced rookie to veteran; on a team of superstars, he was the leader, the captain, a man whose high personal qualities were somehow communicated to the grandstand and bleacher populace. The fence-busting Dodgers of the late 1940s and 1950s were not always popular around the league, but as one writer said,

● *Reese: "Big League from Day One."*

"The one guy you never heard booed, no matter where he played, was Reese."

The man known as Pee Wee was born Harold Henry Reese, on a farm near the village of Ekron, Kentucky, about 40 miles down the Ohio River from Louisville and about a dozen miles west of the nation's bullion repository at Fort Knox. The nickname "Pee Wee" always implied a modest physique, but Reese eventually grew up to five feet ten inches and 160 agile and trimly muscled pounds. Actually, the nickname had nothing to do with his physical dimensions but had derived from a marble called a "pee wee," which the boy Reese shot with championship skills. Still, he wasn't much over 110 pounds when he graduated high school and was hired by the Kentucky Telephone Company as a cable splicer. He became a weekend ballplayer and put on weight, and after a couple of years, was signed out of a Presbyterian Church League

by the Louisville Colonels of the American Association, one of the top minor leagues.

One writer said of Louisville's new recruit, "He looked like he was twelve years old. He had the most boyish, most innocent face. But when he got out of the field, he played like a veteran. He had the surest baseball instincts of any kid shortstop I ever saw. And that wasn't just my opinion. That was everybody's opinion."

Reese was nineteen years old when he made his debut with Louisville, batting .277. Soon he became known as "The Little Colonel," and attracted the attention of major league scouts.

"He was big league from Day One," said one scout, while another added, "The fans love him."

There were two "can't miss" players in the American Association in 1938: Reese and a young slugger with a whiplash swing at Minneapolis named Ted Williams, who was tearing apart the league with the same kind of hitting he was soon to inflict upon the American League. The Boston Red Sox owned Williams, and when they bought the Louisville franchise for around $200,000, they also owned Reese. (One writer said, "five thousand was for the franchise, and the rest was for the kid at short.")

After a second year at Louisville, Reese was ready for the big leagues. However, it would not be with the Red Sox, whose manager Joe Cronin went to Louisville to have a look at Reese. Cronin was not just Boston's manager, he was also its shortstop. According to the story that has become part of baseball lore, Cronin took one look at Reese and realized the boy would put an end to his own, Cronin's, career as a shortstop. Cronin always strenuously denied the story, but Reese was soon sold to the Brooklyn Dodgers. However the story is interpreted, the Boston skipper comes out on the short end, because he either refused to move aside for Reese, or he determined that Pee Wee was not big-league material.

Interestingly, when Reese reported to the Brooklyn Dodgers spring camp in 1940, he joined a club also managed by its shortstop, Leo Durocher, who, like Cronin, was near the end

● *Leo Durocher. One look at Reese and he called it a career.*

of his playing days. Unlike Cronin, however, Leo sized up the rookie and effusively announced that the Dodgers had a new shortstop.

Durocher, one of the fine fielding shortstops of his time, made Reese a personal project, although as Leo conceded, "There wasn't much the kid didn't know. He could play the position like a veteran and he did it with style. And he was such a nice kid, too. Everybody was crazy about him."

Reese's first year in Brooklyn, during which he batted .272, consisted of just 84 games. First, he suffered a severe beaning in Chicago and was out of the lineup for three weeks. Then, in August, he broke a bone in his foot and missed the rest of the season.

In 1941, the Dodgers brought Brooklyn its first pennant in 21 years, outlasting the St. Louis Cardinals in a summer-long pennant race of almost suffocating intensity. For Reese, ironically, it was the worst of his big-league seasons—a .229 batting average and a league-leading 47 errors. Despite this, Leo insisted on playing his young shortstop right on through the pennant race.

"We wanted him out there," said Dodger right-hander Kirby Higbe. "He may have made his errors, but he always made the big play. And there was never a shortstop better at going down the left-field foul line to get a pop fly. You sometimes thought you had four outfielders out there."

Reese led National League shortstops in putouts in 1941 and again in 1942 (as well as assists that year), when the Dodgers played out another classic pennant race with the Cardinals (this time St. Louis won). After the 1942 season, Reese entered the United States Navy, in which he spent the next three years.

"He went away a boy," Durocher said, "and came back a man."

In the spring of 1947, the twenty-nine-year-old Reese, the natural leader on a team brimming with future young superstars, was suddenly put in an awkward situation. He had always been known as an extremely likable and decent young man, and now he found his character being put to trial.

In October 1945, the Dodgers signed Jackie Robinson to a contract with their minor-league affiliate at Montreal, thus breaching baseball's long-standing color barrier. In 1946 Robinson performed sensationally at Montreal, and in the spring of 1947, his promotion to the Brooklyn roster became simply a matter of paper shuffling.

From the perspective of his friends in Kentucky, Reese was faced with a dilemma: to play or not to play alongside a black man. For Reese, however, there was no dilemma. When the subject of what his friends back home might say about him being a teammate of Robinson's, Pee

● *The infield of the pennant-winning 1941 Brooklyn Dodgers. Left to right: third baseman Cookie Lavagetto, shortstop Pee Wee Reese, second baseman Billy Herman, and first baseman Dolf Camilli.*

Jackie Robinson holding the plaque he was awarded for the National League's Most Valuable Player in 1949.

Wee conceded that some of them probably wouldn't like it, but, "I say to hell with anyone who doesn't like it. I don't even know this fellow Robinson; haven't met him; but I do know that he deserves a chance, same as anybody else."

But not everyone felt like Reese, certainly not everyone on the Brooklyn Dodgers, a team whose star players featured uncompromising, tradition-bound southerners like Dixie Walker, Hugh Casey, and Kirby Higbe, who were only the most prominent of the disaffected.

A petition was circulated in the Dodger clubhouse during spring training. It stated that the undersigned refused to play with Robinson. Reese would not sign it, telling the members of the cabal that "you've got your views and I've got mine." Joining Reese were little-known

rookies Gil Hodges and Duke Snider and veterans Eddie Stanky and Pete Reiser, among others; but it was the refusal of the man from Kentucky, the club's highly respected shortstop, that carried, in the words of one newspaperman "a ton of weight." Reese's stand helped put a quick end to the incipient rebellion.

In one well-documented incident, Robinson was taking a brutal hiding from the opposition bench when Reese walked over to his teammate in the middle of the diamond. Reese contrived what appeared to be a brief strategy conference and, while doing so, casually put his hand on Robinson's shoulder for a moment. The gesture silenced the bench jockeys.

"It wasn't just that a teammate did that," Hodges said. "It was that the teammate was Reese. Pee Wee generated that kind of respect."

Robinson never forgot Reese's acceptance of him during those difficult early days of Jackie's career. For his part, Reese never thought he had done anything remarkable, once telling Jackie, "All I did was treat you like I did anyone else."

Robinson laughed. "That," he said, "was probably the best thing you could have done."

Reese and Robinson soon became one of the top double-play combinations in baseball and, along with Hodges, Snider, Billy Cox, Carl Furillo, and Roy Campanella, formed the powerful nucleus of the team that dominated the National League from 1947 through 1956. Winning six pennants and finishing second three times, the Dodgers finally won that cherished World Series in 1955.

Among this team of stars and strong personalities, Reese was the acknowledged leader, the man who made the big plays, delivered clutch hits, and counseled his pitchers in tough situations. The man who at Louisville had been "The Little Colonel" became "The Captain" in Brooklyn; in the context of baseball, it was a significant promotion.

In a rare demonstration of affection, the Dodgers threw a party at Ebbets Field for Reese on the occasion of his 37th birthday, on July 23, 1955. Before the game, Pee Wee received some

● *The core of Brooklyn's great teams in the 1950s.*
Left to right: outfielder Duke Snider, first
baseman Gil Hodges, second baseman Jackie
Robinson, shortstop Pee Wee Reese, and catcher
Roy Campanella.

$20,000 worth of gifts from the team, team-mates, and fans, and in the fifth inning the lights were dimmed while 35,000 fans lit candles and sang "Happy Birthday."

"For the right guy and the right occasion," one writer said, "there can be a hell of a lot of sentiment in baseball."

Nice guy notwithstanding, Reese had earned his accolades with year after year of steady play on the diamonds of the National League. Only once between 1946 and 1955 did his average go below .270, and in 1954 he achieved a career peak of .309. And all the time he kept making all the plays at shortstop with style and deceptive ease

● *Reese in 1956.*

and doing it so routinely for so long that the Milwaukee Braves manager Charlie Grimm once said, "You tend to forget just how good he is."

In 1957, Reese made his concession to time and began appearing more frequently at third base than at short. A year later, the Dodgers moved to Los Angeles, taking their captain with them. Reese played infrequently in 1958, his final year in the majors. He coached for the Dodgers in 1959, then went into broadcasting and later worked for the Louisville Slugger company, which manufactures bats.

In 1984 the achievements of the colonel turned captain were officially noted when Reese was elected to the Hall of Fame.

• • •

Marty Marion.
National Baseball Library, Cooperstown, NY.

MARTY MARION

In those years—the early and middle 1930s, young ballplayers came to the St. Louis Cardinal tryout camps from all corners of the Depression-blighted land. Traveling by bus, rail, freight car, or thumbing rides with trucks and jalopies, they came carrying in one small tidy packet their gloves, spikes, and dreams. At one time in the 1930s, the Cardinals had the most abundantly stocked and far-flung farm system ever in baseball: some 50 teams and 800 players at its peak.

With so much talent crowding the Cardinal organization, life at the top—with the big team in St. Louis—was not as secure as with most other teams. No matter how good you were, there was likely to be somebody younger and hungrier and just as good pushing their way to your job. Even such top guns (and future Hall of Famers) as Joe Medwick and Johnny Mize would be traded to make way for the pure bloods of the thundering herd. But there was one position on the Cardinal squad that, once filled in 1940, remained securely filled and unchallenged for the length of the decade.

"We were always looking for more and more talent, no matter the position," one Cardinal

scout said, "but when Marty Marion came along we knew that we had shortstop locked up for a long time. There just wasn't anybody who was going to do it any better."

In an age when there were shortstops named Luke Appling and Lou Boudreau and Pee Wee Reese, the man they called "Mr. Shortstop" was Martin Whiteford Marion of the St. Louis Cardinals. They also called him "Slats," which probably had something to do with his lanky 6'2" frame. And they also called him "The Octopus," because it seemed he must have had eight limbs in order to cover so much middle-infield real estate and pick up so many ground balls about to become base hits. He was the tallest shortstop in the league, and with his long arms and extraordinary quickness, it made you wonder, as one writer said, "If the Cardinals really needed second and third basemen when Marion was out there."

Marion was born on December 1, 1917, at Richburg, South Carolina, a small town in the north-central part of the state. He was one of four brothers to go into professional baseball. His older brother John had two brief stints with the Washington Senators, a club that had the chance to possess young Marty as well, if not for the team's tight-fisted pecuniary habits.

Marty was signed by Washington's Chattanooga farm club in 1935. The seventeen-year-old boy was told to stick around and watch and learn. One day his girlfriend (whom he later married) came to town, and Marty asked the club secretary Cal Griffith, Jr., for a pass to the game for her. Griffith refused, and an offended Marion quit and went home.

Later that summer, Marion journeyed to Rome, Georgia, to attend a Cardinal tryout camp. The slender teenager made enough of an impression to earn an invitation to St. Louis to work out with the Cardinals. Frankie Frisch, then managing St. Louis's famous "Gashouse Gang," remembered Marion.

"He was the lousiest hitter I ever saw," Frisch said, "but he was a major-league shortstop even then, a master fielder."

The Cardinals offered Marion a contract for around $75 a month, which he took home with him unsigned. At the time, he was a freshman studying mechanical drawing at Georgia Tech. While he was pondering the contract, a persuasive phone call from St. Louis finally induced him to sign, and Marty Marion went off to pro ball.

The following year, Marion began a four-year apprenticeship in the Cardinal organization, the last three of which he was posted at the team's top farm club at Rochester, in the International League. In 1940 he made the big team.

Speaking on behalf of the Cardinal pitching staff, right-hander Lon Warneke said, "We were waiting for them to bring him up. We'd seen him in spring training and we knew what he could do. They said he was a light hitter, but frankly, we didn't care what he hit—we wanted him out there at shortstop."

As a matter of fact, Marion proved to carry more than his weight at bat, punching out a .278 batting average in his rookie year.

● *"Mr. Shortstop."*

Branch Rickey, St. Louis general manager at the time, said "We would have played him even if he had hit 50 points lower; but for a boy with his defensive abilities to hit like that made him a prince among ballplayers."

Marion soon became the infield glue on one of the most successful teams in National League history. Raised almost in its entirety from the Cardinal farm system, they had been trained as one and they played with a spirited aggressiveness and *esprit de corps* that remains unsurpassed among baseball teams. Led by Marion, Stan Musial, Enos Slaughter, Terry Moore, and a wealth of talented pitching, the Cardinals never finished worse than second between 1941 and 1949, and won pennants in 1942, 1943, 1944, and 1946.

● *The outfield of the St. Louis Cardinals' 1942 pennant winners. Left to right: Enos Slaughter, Terry Moore, and Stan Musial.*

By the mid-1940s, Marion's glovework was being ranked with that of Honus Wagner. When someone asked Honus, then a coach with the Pirates, if Marion was indeed as good a shortstop as he had been, the whimsical old boy answered, "I don't know. I never saw myself play." But as someone remarked when asked if they thought Bob Feller was as fast as Walter Johnson, "It doesn't make much difference. Just asking the question is enough. That tells you all you need to know." Connie Mack, who had been watching baseball ever since they decided to make the ball round, offered this opinion in 1944: "There is no doubt in my mind that Marion is the greatest living shortstop, perhaps the greatest of all time."

It was in 1944 that Marion helped the Cardinals to a third straight pennant and participation in the only all-St. Louis World Series ever played. That year the St. Louis Browns won the

● *Cardinal second baseman Red Schoendienst (left) and Marion.*

one pennant they would take in their half-century American League history. Years later, Browns manager Luke Sewell recalled his team's six-game loss to the Cardinals:

"The memory I carried away with me most vividly from that Series," Sewell said, "is Marion at shortstop: diving, lunging, scooping, covering an unbelievable amount of ground. But not only did he play an outstanding defensive game, after awhile he began to demoralize our hitters.

They were smacking balls that should have been base hits, and with any other shortstop out there, would have been base hits, but he kept gobbling them up. Once you begin thinking that somebody on the opposing team is invincible, it begins to diminish your own game."

Marion indeed played well in the 1944 series, handling 29 chances without an error. That fall, his brilliant infield play earned him further distinction when he became the first shortstop ever to win a Most Valuable Player

● *Chicago White Sox manager Marty Marion
(right) breaking in his rookie shortstop Luis
Aparicio in the spring of 1956.*

Award. When a man who bats .267, with just six
home runs and 63 runs batted in, wins MVP
honors, it tells you he is doing something on that
field as well as it possibly can be done.

Marion remained "Mr. Shortstop" until
1950, when nagging back problems forced him
to the sidelines at the age of 32. At this point he
began a second career, as manager. Taking over
the Cardinals in 1951, he brought them in third,
but was discharged at the end of the year. He
then managed the St. Louis Browns in 1952 and
1953, finishing seventh and eighth, which were
standard terminal points for the Browns in those

years. He returned to the active rolls with the
Browns in 1952 and got into 67 games. In 1953
Marion quit for good after two games at third
base; it was the only time in his professional
career that he played anywhere but the position
that had given him his prestigious nickname.

Marion managed the Chicago White Sox in
1955 and 1956, turning in respectable third-place
finishes each year. In 1956, his final year in uniform, Marion's rookie shortstop was Luis Aparicio. In baseball's timeless relay of star coming
after star, it was an appropriate passing of the
baton.

Chicago Cubs rookie Ernie Banks in 1953.
National Baseball Library, Cooperstown, NY.

ERNIE BANKS

In the late 1950s and early 1960s, there were two shortstops in the city of Chicago, one with the White Sox and the other with the Cubs. Their names were Luis Aparicio, whose sleight-of-hand defensive work dazzled the fans at Comiskey Park, and Ernie Banks, whose wrist-snap swing produced offensive statistics unprecedented (and unequaled) for a shortstop.

Banks played only eight years at shortstop, but during that time, he had his greatest success, building a solid foundation for his Hall of Fame career. Five times he hit 40 or more home runs, and in 1958 and 1959, he was voted the National League's Most Valuable Player.

Bank's congenial nature and sunny disposition earned him a reputation as one of baseball's "nice guys." Despite spending his entire career playing on what were for the most part losing teams (he never made it to the World Series), Banks never lost his enthusiasm for the game. His credo, "Let's play two today," became as well known as his lusty hitting.

Jackie Robinson's pioneering path to the major leagues in 1947 was hardly well-traveled when Ernie Banks walked it straight from the Negro League to Wrigley Field in 1953. The first black to play for the Cubs, the twenty-two-year-old Banks was a rangily built six-footer with wrists that seemed constructed from supple steel.

"He hit what I like to call 'sudden' home runs," said Stan Hack, who managed Banks during Ernie's break-in years. "He'd take that quick swing and *bam!*—the ball would be off on a high line drive right into the seats. Home run. Just like that."

Banks was born in Dallas, Texas, on January 31, 1931. It was a vintage year for home run hitters, as Willie Mays, Mickey Mantle, and Eddie Mathews were also born that year. It was Ernie's father Eddie, a former semi-pro player around Dallas, who gently encouraged the boy's interest in baseball. Ernie had been devoting his athletic interests to football, basketball, softball, and track.

"He never insisted I play ball," Ernie said. "But I loved my father and I knew that it made him happy when I played, so

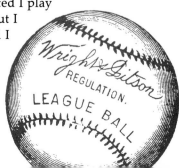

naturally I did. He never pushed me, but he had his way of getting me out there."

Eddie Banks scraped together a few Depression-era dollars and bought his son a glove. "Then," Ernie recalled, "he'd give me a couple of nickels to go out and play catch with him."

The spark ignited by his father soon began burning on its own talent. The slim youngster became a sandlot star and then a high school star. Upon graduation in 1951, Banks was signed by the Kansas City Monarchs, one of the top teams of the Negro League and the same team which had sent Jackie Robinson into organized ball just a few years before.

"Ernie was a major-league prospect from the day he reported to the Monarchs," club owner Tom Baird said. "He hit the long ball and he fielded brilliantly."

Though no one was going at it with sledgehammers, the big-league color barrier was beginning to crumble. In 1953, six years after Robinson's big-league debut, only three of the eight National League clubs (the Brooklyn Dodgers, New York Giants, and Boston Braves) had employed black players. The Chicago Cubs were about to become the fourth.

After having scouted Banks during the 1953 season, the Cubs were convinced he was not only a prospect, but ready to step right into their lineup. After purchasing him from the Monarchs late in the season, the Cubs flew Ernie straight to Chicago, and on September 17, 1953, the man who would become known as "Mr. Cub" began his career.

There were ten games remaining on the schedule and Banks got into them all, batting .314 and hitting the first two of his 512 career home runs. The Cubs were more than satisfied, and Ernie played in 424 consecutive games from the start of his career, a major-league record.

Full-fledged stardom came to Banks in 1955, his second full season. Not only did he set a major-league record for shortstops, with 44 home runs, he also led in fielding (.972). He drove in 117 runs and batted .295 and, for a bit of icing, set another record (since broken) by hitting five grand slam home runs.

Looking back at that 1955 season, one sees that the National League was in a Golden Age of slugging talent. In Brooklyn there was Gil Hodges, Roy Campanella, and Duke Snider; in New York, Willie Mays; in Milwaukee, Hank Aaron and Eddie Mathews; in Cincinnati, Ted Kluszewski; in St. Louis, the league's best all-around hitter, Stan Musial; and now in Chicago, Ernie Banks.

"He made the fans proud to come out to Wrigley Field," Stan Hack said. "We were a second-division team but all of a sudden we had one of the best players in baseball."

Banks was indeed one of the best, and he was going to get better. In 1957 he whacked 43 homers and drove in 102 runs. Then in 1958 he broke his own record for shortstops with 47 home runs and drove in a league-leading 129 runs while batting .313. This performance earned him the Most Valuable Player Award. A year later he was even better. He busted 45 home runs, led with a mammoth 143 RBIs, and committed just 12 errors while setting a record (since broken) with a .985 fielding average. It added up to a second straight MVP designation.

"I could have sworn," Dodger manager Walter Alston said facetiously, "that somewhere in the rule book it says that shortstops aren't supposed to hit like that."

No shortstop, before or since, ever hit with the long-ball authority of Banks, and it was inevitable that Ernie's lethal hitting would overshadow his defensive work. To some people, a shortstop who led the league in home runs and runs batted in simply had to have serious defensive shortcomings, but the fact was that Banks was more than an able glove man. In only eight seasons as a shortstop, he led in putouts once, assists twice, and fielding three times.

According to Stan Hack, Ernie had "tremendously quick hands and sharp reflexes" that made it almost impossible for a ball to "bad hop" him.

● *The greatest slugging shortstop in baseball history.*

"Excellent range and great hands," was Walter Alston's opinion of Banks.

"Naturally you don't hear much about Ernie's fielding," Pirate manager Danny Murtaugh said. "When his name comes up all you hear about is his hitting. But he looks pretty damned good to me out in the field. He may not have the strongest arm in the league, but no shortstop is more accurate."

Cincinnati manager Mayo Smith probably put it most definitively when he said, "All I know is that the Cubs put him out there at shortstop every year for every game." (While playing shortstop, Banks led the National League six times in games played.)

In 1962, an injured knee made it difficult for Banks to pivot quickly, and the Cubs were forced to move him to first base. He soon adapted to the position without too much difficulty.

Banks never hit quite as thunderously as a first baseman as he had as a shortstop, his home run peaks being 37 in 1962 and 32 in 1968. But for the years he played shortstop, the 277 home runs he hit remain the major league record for the position.

The closest the Cubs came to winning a pennant while Banks was on the team was in 1969, when after a strong summer's play, the team collapsed in September and watched the "Miracle Mets" go charging past them. The thirty-eight-year-old Banks delivered 106 RBIs that year, which was the eighth and final time he cleared the 100 mark in RBIs. It was also his last full season.

After 72 games in 1970 and 39 the following year, he retired. His 512 career home runs tie him with Mathews for fifth place on the all-time National League scroll.

Banks's popularity in Chicago soared during his great years, and fan affection for him never faltered. He became "Mr. Cub," and "the most

● *Banks firing to first to complete a double play.*

popular Cub player of all time," thanks to his powerhouse slugging and an endearing personality that was unfailingly cheerful and optimistic. His popularity in Chicago was so compelling, in fact, that, paradoxically, there was once a movement underfoot among certain Cub fans to have him traded to a contender so he might have the opportunity to play in a World Series.

"The riches of the game," Banks once said, "are in the thrills, not the money."

Banks enjoyed the greatest thrill his game had to offer in 1977, when he was elected to baseball's Hall of Fame.

● *"Mr. Cub."*

Luis Aparicio.

LUIS APARICIO

Across 18 major league seasons, Luis Aparicio never played any position other than shortstop.

"Where else would you have put him?" asked his one-time manager Al Lopez. "And why?"

Indeed. By the time he retired in 1973, with the all-time record for shortstops of 2,581 games at the position, Aparicio was almost universally acknowledged as having had no superior as a defensive player.

"He's making his plays with the lively ball," said Casey Stengel. "Ain't nobody in my time who could do that unless maybe Hans Wagner, and he was around in the lump-of-coal days. I've seen them all, played with some of them— Bancroft, Maranville, Marion, Boudreau, Rizzuto—never seen anybody make the plays this little man does. And with the lively ball, too. Don't forget that. One of these days you'll see that Aparicio field a ball in back of the pitcher and out-run the hitter to first base. He's done everything else, ain't he?"

According to one American Leaguer, a contemporary of Aparicio's, Luis was on the batter's mind "as much as the pitcher was. Sometimes you might top a ball just past the third-base side of the mound, or hit one deep into the hole on the left side, and you'd start running like hell because you knew you had a chance to beat it out. But then you remembered who was out there: Aparicio. So you tried to run harder, because you knew that he got to a ball a split second faster than anybody else, that he would get it away quicker than anybody else, and that his arm was strong and accurate. When you left the batter's box you thought you might have a hit, but when you crossed first base you saw the umpire's thumb in the air."

Aparicio was born April 29, 1934, in Maracaibo, an oil-producing city on the northwest coast of Venezuela. His father, Luis, Sr., had earned national esteem as a shortstop, playing for nearly two decades on the professional

● *Chico Carrasquel, Aparicio's boyhood idol and predecessor as White Sox shortstop.*

diamonds of Venezuela. And there are those who still maintain that the greatest shortstop to come out of Venezuela was not Chico Carrasquel, Luis Aparicio, Jr., or Dave Concepcion, but Luis Aparicio, Sr.

Always avid about baseball, young Luis would sometimes slip out onto the field and take infield practice with his father's team. "I remember when he was only nine or ten years old," Carrasquel said. "Some pretty hot smashes were hit his way, and he always got in front of them. He was never afraid."

It was more than desire and the raw impulses of burgeoning talent that rooted the boy in front of hard-hit ground balls; Luis worshipped his father and strove to emulate him. So it was a highly emotional moment when young Luis turned professional with his father's team,

the Maracaibo Gavilanes, on November 18, 1953, for the day also marked his father's retirement. After Luis, Sr., played the first ball hit to him, the game was stopped while he walked off the field and his son walked on. As their paths crossed in the middle of the infield, the father handed his glove to his son. "It was a touching and truly beautiful moment," one writer said.

When Aparicio began exhibiting his dazzling range, quickness, and strong throwing arm on the hard-baked infields of Maracaibo, Caracas, and the other ports of call of the Venezuelan winter league, the big league scouts began to crowd in on him. Despite having Carrasquel, the White Sox resolved they would not be outbid for Aparicio.

"As good as Chico was," White Sox general manager Frank Lane said, "we knew that Luis was going to be better."

The White Sox got their man, thus assuring themselves of more than three decades of stellar continuity at shortstop. From 1930 to 1962, Luke Appling, Carrasquel, and Aparicio held the infield's key position for the club.

Aparicio entered organized ball with the Waterloo, Iowa, club of the Three-Eye League in 1954. There he batted .282 and entertained the customers in the small farm towns with a brand of glovework that was already big league. The White Sox polished their jewel at Memphis in the Southern Association the following year. There he batted .273 but led shortstops with 44 errors.

"That didn't bother us," one White Sox scout said of Luis's high error total. "He was getting his glove on balls he had no business reaching in the first place and was being nicked with errors for his trouble."

The White Sox were so sure of their twenty-one-year-old minor leaguer that right after the 1955 season they traded Carrasquel, opening the way for Aparicio to succeed the man who had been one of his idols.

When he joined the White Sox in 1956, the 5'8", 140-pound rookie had a tendency to give ground at second base when burly baserunners

● *Nelson Fox.*

came roaring in to break up a double play. White Sox manager Marty Marion, the best shortstop of his day and one who had learned his baseball along the rugged byways of the St. Louis Cardinal farm system, pulled Luis aside and gave him the definitive word on how to deal with intimidating baserunners.

"If the runner is coming right at you," Marion said, "just make your peg as if he's not there. Do that and I guarantee you, he won't be there."

Coming to Comiskey Park, Aparicio teamed with veteran second baseman Nelson Fox to form one of baseball's all-time keystone combinations. In five of the seven years they played together, they helped the White Sox lead in team fielding.

"Outside of advising him how to play certain hitters," Fox said, "there wasn't much I could tell him. He was the most fully equipped

shortstop I ever saw and had natural baseball instincts. He was also a nice kid, sweet-tempered, always smiling, and modest. And he never changed."

Aparicio was everything the White Sox hoped he would be, batting a respectable .266, leading league shortstops in putouts and assists (this was the first of six consecutive years he led in this latter category, which was a major-league record), and the near-unanimous choice for American League Rookie of the Year, winning 22 of a possible 24 votes.

The new man also led in stolen bases (21) for the first of nine consecutive years in which he topped the league in thefts, which is the major-league record. When Aparicio broke in, the stolen base was still a neglected art form. In 1959, he stole 56 bases, which was more than twice the total of any other big-league player and more than the total of six American League teams.

Sparked by Aparicio and Fox, whose non-stop hustle helped earn the team the nickname "Go-Go Sox," the White Sox ended a forty-year drought and were the surprising American League pennant winners in 1959, upsetting a New York Yankee team that was in the midst of taking 14 pennants in 16 years.

This was the year that Aparicio began a string of eight straight years leading league shortstops in fielding. He shares this record with Everett Scott.

In January 1963, White Sox fans learned to their surprise and dismay that the best shortstop in the league had been traded to the Baltimore Orioles as part of a six-player swap.

At Baltimore, Aparicio teamed up with third baseman Brooks Robinson, creating what was probably the most airtight left side of any infield in baseball history. (Aparicio played five years for the Orioles, and four times he and Robinson each led in fielding at their respective positions.)

"Nothing got through there," lamented Detroit manager Chuck Dressen. "They made the hard plays, the easy plays, all the plays. The only

● *Luis Aparicio, who was according to Nelson Fox, "The most fully equipped shortstop I ever saw."*

● *Aparicio with the Baltimore Orioles in 1964.*

thing that got into left field was a ball hit in the air, and even that had to be at least ten feet off the ground."

In 1966, Aparicio got into his second World Series and helped cement the Los Angeles Dodgers in four straight. The Baltimore pitchers held the Dodgers to two runs and a .142 batting average, while the Oriole defense did not commit a single error.

In November 1967, Aparicio, now thirty-three years old, was traded back to the White Sox, for whom he played until 1970. In his last year there, he recorded a .313 batting average, the only time he reached .300 in his 18-year career over which he averaged .262.

In 1970, there were rumors that he would be named White Sox manager, but instead, in December, Aparicio was traded to the Boston Red

Sox. He played out his big-league career with Boston and retired after the 1973 season at the age of thirty-nine.

Among Aparicio's array of lifetime major-league records were most games for a shortstop (2,518), most assists (8,016), most chances accepted (12,564), most double plays (1,553), and the American League record for most putouts (4,548). In addition he had season-by-season fielding and stolen-base records.

It all finally added up to his election to baseball's Hall of Fame in 1984. The news of Aparicio's election to baseball's most hallowed corridors reached Maracaibo during a ball game at the city's stadium and was excitedly announced over the public address system. The crowd rose and gave a loud, sustained roar of approval.

● *Boston Red Sox shortstop Luis Aparicio firing to first base on a double play attempt. Detroit's Eddie Brinkman is the man on the ground, and Dick McAuliffe the baserunner.*

Dave Concepcion.

National Baseball Library, Cooperstown, NY.

DAVE CONCEPCION

You can be a distinguished veteran player, a potential Hall of Famer, with an array of Gold Glove awards decorating your den, but you never lose your respect for the challenges of the job, a job that can consume the nonchalant and the unprepared no matter how refined their skills. Until the time he retired, Dave Concepcion took eighty ground balls every day, having them hit to every precinct of his infield domain: ground balls that were sharp, that went deep, that were topped. Concepcion prepared for the unexpected and kept his skills sharp for the expected. This dedication does not necessarily make someone a great shortstop, but if he already is one, so he will remain.

Concepcion was at shortstop for the Cincinnati Reds for almost two decades (1970–1988). Most notably, he was a key member of "The Big Red Machine" championship teams of the 1970s, perhaps the most eminent aggregation of talent in National League history. Some people felt that playing among such stars as Johnny Bench, Pete Rose, Joe Morgan, George Foster, and Tony Perez, Concepcion tended to be overlooked. Manager Sparky Anderson disagreed.

"Don't you believe it," the skipper said. "The pitcher always knew where he was, and that's where they tried to get the ball hit. He's one of the few shortstops that when the ball is hit to him with two out, I've seen pitchers start heading for the dugout without looking back."

Concepcion's play at shortstop was so fluid that the nickname "Immaculate Concepcion" was inevitably pinned to him. "He looks like he's playing on roller skates," Anderson said.

The man who was to become the idol of a generation of Latin-American shortstops was born David Ismael Concepcion, on June 17, 1948, in Aragua, a small town inland from Venezuela's east coast. He was brought up in nearby Maracay, about thirty miles east of Caracas. As a youngster, David began heeding the coercive impulses of talent by playing with rubber balls and wooden sticks that were hand-carved to resemble bats. His greatest love, then and later, came in indulging his natural ability for taking control of a batted ball. The

● *Dave Concepcion: "Yeah, we knew we had a shortstop there."*

feeling, he said, was "indescribable," like "when you hit the ball on the sweet part of the bat or when you make love."

David's father, a talented semi-pro ball-player, wanted his son to go to college and get an education. The young man did attend Augustin Codazzi College in Aragua, but by the time he was nineteen, Concepcion had made a reputation playing semi-pro ball and attracted the attention of Cincinnati scout Wilfredo Calvino, who signed him to a contract in 1968. There was no bonus. "Not a centavo," Concepcion said, but the rewards would come later, in 1981, when the Reds made him baseball's first million-dollar shortstop. (The Reds let Morgan, Rose, and Foster go because of free agency, but made sure they retained Concepcion, for whom, they said, "There was no replacement.")

"He was beautiful to watch in the field, right from the first," a Cincinnati scout said of the young Venezuelan who reported to the team's minor league complex in Tampa in 1968. "He had a shortstop's build, an inch or two over six feet and around 155 pounds. He moved with a lot of grace and had enormous range, getting to

everything and then whipping the ball on a line to first, throwing strikes. Yeah, we knew we had a shortstop there."

The young man who would be named to nine National League All-Star teams and who would win five Gold Gloves was lonely and homesick during that first spring training. Unable to speak English, he would go to restaurants with teammates and when he had to order, he would repeat what the man before him had asked for.

Concepcion never forgot the feeling of being a stranger away from home. Years later, when he was a star, he would occasionally wander over to the club's minor-league complex during spring training. Seeking out the Latin players, he would make sure they were getting on all right and understood what was expected of them.

Concepcion played for the Tampa club in the Florida State League in 1968, moved up to Asheville in the Southern League in 1969, and finished out the year with the Red's top farm club at Indianapolis in the American Association, where he batted .341 in 42 games. The following year he joined the Reds, launching the career that would earn for him status as a national hero, as it had for his Venezuelan predecessors Chico Carrasquel and Luis Aparicio.

After batting .260 in his first season and helping the Reds to a pennant, Concepcion suffered a thumb injury in spring training the next year and labored through a .205 season. Things weren't much better in 1972, when he batted .209. But the Reds were building a powerful club and they felt they could carry a glove as smooth as Concepcion's, no matter how little he hit.

A year later, however, the club discovered it not only had a good defensive shortstop, but one who suddenly fit into the potent lineup around him. When Concepcion went down for the rest of the season with a broken ankle in late July 1973, he was batting .287. It was not a fluke; for eight of the next nine years he batted .271 or better, including .301 in 1978 and .306 in 1981. In 1979 he achieved personal highs with 16 home runs and 84 runs batted in.

● *Four members of "The Big Red Machine." Left to right, first baseman Tony Perez, catcher Johnny Bench, second baseman Joe Morgan, and third baseman Pete Rose.*

In 1979, a writer asked Pee Wee Reese to evaluate the top shortstops of the day. "Mark Belanger is exceptionally smooth," Reese said. "Larry Bowa is very quick. Rick Burleson is a fiery leader. Bill Russell has an accurate arm. But no one does everything as well as Dave Concepcion."

Like DiMaggio in center field, Concepcion was a high-style player, graceful and with a bit of flash. He could make easy plays seem difficult and hard ones silken smooth. Occasionally he provoked mock barking from the opposing dugout, a good-natured sound implying there was a "hot dog" on the field.

If he was superstitious, then this, too, was in the Concepcion style; he chose to wear uniform number 13 (the Ohio license plate on his red Mercedes bore the marker "DC13SS"). Once, fighting a batting slump, he decided to take a pre-game shower in full uniform to wash out the gremlins. On another occasion, troubled by another slump, he walked from the ball park to his hotel wearing white shirt, tie, suit jacket, and baseball pants, hoping that this sartorial mismatch would help dispel the problem.

The young man who had come to the big leagues shy and wide-eyed soon became a relaxed and sometimes whimsical character (the Reds helped him immensely by having him room with the club's most popular player, the gregarious Tony Perez). One day, in the visitors' clubhouse at Wrigley Field, he announced that he had a new way of warming up and stepped into the oversized industrial clothes dryer on the premises. A teammate could not resist turning the start button to high speed, and Concepcion's face made several startled, panicky revolutions at the glass door before he was rescued.

"His mouth was wide open," one player said, "and his eyes were bigger than his mouth. When Sparky asked what the hell had been going on, somebody told him that Davey had been trying to shrink his strike zone."

Year after year, Concepcion continued to fence off the shortstop position, gliding back and forth and in and out, punctuating each play with

● *Tony Perez.*

strong, accurate throws. When asked by a sportswriter to describe his favorite play, Concepcion recalled one he hadn't made at shortstop. The play embodied hustle and initiative, and Davey recalled it with pride:

"A fly ball was hit to center field, and Cesar Geronimo lost it in the sun. I saw he couldn't see it, and I ran as fast as I could into center field. With my back to the infield, I caught the ball over my shoulder right where the center fielder normally plays."

It was Concepcion who brought a rare innovation to the conservative old game of baseball. In 1980 he suffered an elbow injury that took some of the strength from his throwing arm. So, when playing on artificial turf, where he had to position himself deeper, he sometimes fired his pegs to first base on one hop. This technique at once eased the strain on his arm, got

● *Dave Concepcion.*

the ball to the bag just as fast, and assured the first baseman of an easy throw to handle. Many shortstops have since emulated the one-bounce throw on artificial turf.

Concepcion completed his 19th and final big-league season in 1988, filling in at every infield position (which he had also done in 1987, when he batted .319 in 104 games).

By the time he retired, Concepcion had played 2,178 games at shortstop, which was fourth on the all-time list and just 44 fewer than National League record-holder Larry Bowa.

Robin Yount, baseball prodigy.

ROBIN YOUNT

Baseball is not a profession known for its prodigies. Among the handful who qualify for the designation is Robin Yount, who not only became a big-league regular at a remarkably young age (eighteen) but did so at the infield's most demanding position.

Yount played shortstop for the Milwaukee Brewers from 1974 to 1984. Then, because of shoulder problems, he switched to center field, a position calling for exceptional defensive skills, and continued his high-caliber play. Yount's all-around play in center was so impressive that in 1989 he won a second Most Valuable Player Award coupling it with the one he received in 1982.

The 1989 award elevated Yount to an elite category; along with Hank Greenberg and Stan Musial, who had each excelled at first base and the outfield, the Milwaukee star became just the third man in baseball history to win MVP honors while playing at different positions.

After the 1989 season, Yount declared free agency. The thought of Yount defecting to another team provoked an astonishing response from Milwaukee civic groups, clubs, organizations, elementary schools, and others. It was as though a beloved family member might be going away. Yount and the Brewers were besieged with pleas and petitions and newspaper editorials, all with the same message: Don't go.

Yount didn't go. Turning down what was reportedly a "blank check" offer from the California Angels, Robin signed another multi-year contract with the Brewers. He said he preferred to stay in Milwaukee because it was "easier to play in than a big media town . . . it's a family city," and because of loyalty to club owner Bud Selig.

It wasn't just Yount's playing skills that appealed to the people of Milwaukee; he was a star player of warmth and modesty, and utterly unaffected by wealth and fame.

"When you hear some players disparaging their own efforts and stressing the team concept," one Milwaukee writer said, "you sometimes find yourself coughing into your hand; but when you hear Robin Yount talk that way, you believe it, because you know the guy and you know it's genuine."

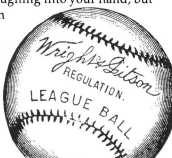

"He's completely unaware of and indifferent to his stats," another writer said, "and I can prove it. Sometime in the middle of the 1982 season, when he was knocking everybody dead with his MVP year, I told him that if he could tell me within five points of what he was batting, I'd make out a check for fifty bucks to his favorite charity. He couldn't do it."

Yount was born on September 16, 1955, at Danville, Illinois, but grew up in Southern California, where the family moved when he was still an infant. He was an all-around athlete at Taft High School, with baseball as his specialty. His older brother Larry (who later became a successful real estate developer in Arizona and Robin's own sharp-minded agent) pitched for several years in the Houston Astros organization. In high school at that time, Robin occasionally spent some school vacation time with Larry, working out with the team, getting a feel for professional baseball, and probably developing the maturity that would soon impress people. This experience helped ease him into the minor leagues when he broke in with Newark of the Class A New York-Pennsylvania League in 1973. The Brewers had made him their first-round draft pick in 1973 (he was number 3 overall).

Getting into 64 games, Yount batted .295 and made a good impression with his glove. One scout described Yount as having "amazing professionalism for a seventeen-year-old."

The Brewers decided to invite him to their spring camp in 1974 for a brief inspection before their minor-league camp opened. They would then decide to which minor-league team he would be assigned. That decision was never made.

One afternoon manager Del Crandall grabbed a fungo bat and called the youngster out of his self-imposed anonymity and told him to "get out there." Crandall began whacking sizzling grass-cutters all over the shortstop position and Yount kept darting to his right and to his left, snatching up everything.

"I was impressed," Crandall said, "and what impressed me even more was that guys on the sidelines stopped what they were doing to watch him."

A few days later, Crandall went to general manager Jim Wilson and said, "What do you think of an eighteen-year-old kid opening for us at shortstop?"

Wilson's response was, "Why not?"

So just a year after graduating high school, Robin Yount was a regular shortstop in the big leagues. The prodigy still had some rough edges to iron out; in his second year, he led league shortstops with 44 errors.

"Remember," one Brewers coach said, "he was growing up at the big-league level, and he made his mistakes. But what I liked about him was he never got flustered; he reacted to his mistakes like a veteran would. He just kept going about his business and getting better. That was the thing everybody liked about the kid—he kept getting better."

As he continued filling out physically, Yount began hitting harder. In 1977 he batted .288, and a year later, .293. In the spring of 1978, the Milwaukee organization held its collective breath when a story broke that Yount, an excellent golfer, was contemplating giving up baseball and joining the pro golf tour. Yount later denied that such a career move had ever entered his mind, saying the story somehow got into the papers and took on a life of its own. Even with Yount's disclaimers, the story will probably remain a part of his history.

In 1980, Yount hit harder than ever before: 23 home runs, a league-leading 49 doubles, and a .293 batting average. In the strike-shortened 1981 season, he led American-League shortstops in fielding. A year later he went from star to superstar.

Yount has a personality split common to many great athletes: modest and unassuming away from the field, but a dynamo of intensity and concentration on the field. These latter qualities erupted in full during 1982, when a

● *Yount about to get his man.*

hard-hitting Milwaukee club put on a drive for the Eastern Division title. In the season's final game, Yount's under-the-gun abilities showed themselves in the raw.

Holding a three-game lead over Baltimore, Milwaukee was on the road for a season-ending four-game series with the Orioles. The Orioles began digging themselves out of their precarious position and took the first three games, putting the two clubs into a deadlock. There was one last game to play and a summer's work riding on it. For the Brewers, a defeat would have been not only painful, but humiliating, too.

It was under these circumstances that Robin Yount went to work, putting the final jewels into the crown of his MVP season. He hit a home run

in his first at bat, then another in his second. Later, he added a triple, leading the club to a 10–2 victory that clinched Milwaukee's first division title.

In the Brewers' seven-game World Series loss to the St. Louis Cardinals, Yount was torrid, rapping out 12 hits for a .414 batting average.

In 1982, the American League's Most Valuable Player batted .331 (losing the batting title by a single point to Kansas City's Willie Wilson), hit 29 home runs, drove in 114 runs, scored 129 runs, and led in hits (210), doubles (46), total bases (367), and slugging (.578). Only two other shortstops in history had ever led in slugging and total bases in the same year—Honus Wagner and Ernie Banks.

● *"He just kept getting better."*

● *Robin Yount: ". . . a dynamo of intensity and concentration."*

In his next two seasons, Yount batted .308 and .298. The 1984 season was Yount's eleventh and last as a shortstop. Plagued by shoulder miseries, he became a center fielder in 1985, making the transition without dropping a stitch. Beginning in 1986, he ran off batting averages of .312, .312, .306, and .318, the last of which helped him to his second MVP Award in 1989.

Baseball fans all over and particularly in Milwaukee have watched Robin Yount grow from poised prodigy to self-assured veteran, a man on course for 3,000 lifetime hits and a place in the Hall of Fame. If not for the injury that moved him to center field after 11 years at shortstop, Robin Yount might have settled once and for all the question of who is the greatest shortstop since Wagner.

● *Robin Yount: MVP shortstop, MVP center fielder.*

Alan Trammell.

ALAN TRAMMELL

A major league pennant race is like a long-distance track event; it calls for pacing and stamina and, at crucial moments, spirited surging. In 1984, however, the Detroit Tigers left the starting blocks on Opening Day as though they were going to run the long event like so many sprinters. For six weeks the Tigers proceeded virtually without hindrance, running up a stunning 35–5 record, and reducing the division race to dust and pebbles in less than a third of the season. In a game that prides itself on built-in checks and balances designed to prevent such things as the Detroit runaway, the team performance was unique in baseball history.

The runaway Tigers club of 1984 was a solid one, though not one ornamented with superstars. Realistically, there was just one potential future Hall of Famer—shortstop Alan Trammell. At age twenty-six and already in his eighth major-league season, the young veteran batted .314 and committed the fewest errors of any shortstop in the league (10).

Detroit's rampaging start in 1984 drew more and more attention to the team and its star players, which, besides Trammell, included outfielder Kirk Gibson, second baseman Lou Whitaker, catcher Lance Parrish, and pitchers Jack Morris and Willie Hernandez. Soon the baseball public at large came to know what American League observers had known for years—at shortstop the Tigers had one of the best to play the position.

Trammell's leap to first-magnitude stardom made people acutely conscious of the fact that the American League was in the midst of a "Golden Age" of stellar shortstops. In 1982, Robin Yount's MVP year had led the Milwaukee Brewers to a pennant, and in 1983, Cal Ripkin's MVP year had done the same for the Baltimore Orioles. By mid-season 1984, the speculation was that for the third year in a row there would be an MVP shortstop on a championship team (the award, however, went to Detroit's relief ace Hernandez).

Born in Garden Grove, California, on February 21, 1958, Trammell grew up in San Diego.

● *Alan Trammell: "He played steady as a rock."*

● *Detroit manager Sparky Anderson.*

From an early age, he was determined to make a career in athletics. An all-around athlete at San Diego's Kearney High School, he was Detroit's surprise second-round pick in the June 1976 amateur free-agent draft. The boy was considered a good prospect but had been seen as a probable sixth- or seventh-round selection.

"It may sound strange," one scout said, recalling the Kearney High youngster, "but his very maturity on the field might have caused us to pass him by. There was nothing flashy about him. Talented high school shortstops usually try to put on an exciting show—especially when they know scouts are in attendance—jumping and diving and showing off their arms. But this Trammell kid, he played steady as a rock. He was the kind of kid that didn't catch your eye, but stayed in your mind."

West Coast scout Dick Wiencek had persuaded the Tigers about Trammell. In his reports, Wiencek said the boy was "very quick in the field at ball contact," "smart . . . knows the game," and "a good candidate for quick promotion if physical ability matches mental skills."

The scout was right on the money, for after a year-and-a-half in the minors, the nineteen-year-old Trammell joined the Tigers at the end of the 1977 season. A year later, he was Detroit's regular shortstop.

Trammell's ascent to stardom, according to Sparky Anderson, who took over as Tiger manager in 1979, was due to increased self-confidence. "In his first year or two," Sparky said, "he was awed by it all. He played on talent, but not with confidence." A few bad outings, Sparky said, would leave the youngster brooding. "But now, he can have two or three bad days in a row and adjust."

An example of Trammell's positive approach to business was shown during the second half of the 1982 season. After batting a wretched .203 by mid-July, he said he could have "taken a nose dive and doubted myself." Instead, Trammell gathered his resources during the All-Star break and resolved "to take my average up ten points at a time." Hitting steadily through the season's second half, Trammell checked in at season's end with a respectable .258 average.

Managing at Kansas City when Trammell came into the American League, Whitey Herzog said the new man "was as good defensively as anybody I've ever seen." Anderson added, "Trammell knows the game. All the little things you teach in instructional leagues came as standard equipment with him. He's a complete package."

The solid Trammell defensive play is based on consistency of approach, derived from the credo "The way you practice is the way you play." In other words, baseball is always to be taken seriously, even during pre-game warmups. "Never go nonchalantly after a ball," he said. "If you do it in batting practice you might do it in a game. Get in front of it and catch it with two hands and then concentrate on the accuracy of your throw." (Trammell has said he tried to model his defensive style after Baltimore's Mark Belanger.)

Trammell gradually surprised everyone with his hitting. In 1980 he batted an even .300; then, after a pair of .258 seasons, he batted .319 in 1983 and .314 in the pennant year. By 1984, Trammell had earned a reputation as one of baseball's toughest clutch hitters. What makes a hitter extremely dangerous in pressure situations has never, and probably cannot, be truly explained. Maybe it is increased concentration, maybe it is athletic expression of "character." Whatever it is, Trammell is one of its exemplars. In Detroit's three-game sweep of the pennant

● *Lou Whitaker.*

playoffs in 1984, he batted .364, and in the club's five-game World Series victory over San Diego, he hit two home runs, drove in six runs, collected nine hits (tying a record for a five-game Series), and batted .450.

Trammell had one more surprise in store for his employers and for the baseball community—home run power. He began targeting the far seats in 1986 when he popped 21 home runs. Then a year later, he increased his home run output with 28 long ones, which were part of his best offensive season and one of the best of any shortstop of recent times: 28 home runs, 105 RBIs, 205 hits, and a .343 batting average. He followed this in 1988 with a fifth .300-plus season (.311).

A large part of the Alan Trammell story in Detroit is his long friendship and infield partnership with second baseman Lou Whitaker. They began playing together with Montgomery in the Southern Association in 1977. Both joined the Tigers that September to begin the longest-running double play duo in baseball history, providing a combination of crackling hitting and snappy defense.

"There's nothing out there that they can't do," Kansas City manager Dick Howser said. "You can't beat them on cutoffs, relays, pickoffs, getting and passing along defensive signals, and covering ground."

When each club's all-time all-star team is put together, few lineups can match the illustrious names put forth by the Tigers: Ty Cobb, Harry Heilmann, Hank Greenberg, Charlie Gehringer, Al Kaline, Harvey Kuenn, Jim Bunning, Lance Parrish, Jack Morris. Fires of controversy may burn here and there about certain positions, but not about shortstop. Alan Trammell, as good as any during the American League's "Golden Age" of shortstops, is the best man the Detroit Tigers have ever posted at that position.

● *Alan Trammell on deck.*

• • •

Ozzie Smith: "When I go out on the field I'm
in my own world."

OZZIE SMITH

W hen I go out on the field," Ozzie Smith said, "I'm in my own world. I feel like there are no restrictions, no limitations. It's just free and easy, and I let it flow."

These feelings and impulses are most frequently associated with creative people, but upon the athletic fields of his time, Ozzie Smith of the St. Louis Cardinals has played not only with response and intuition but with imagination, too.

Ozzie Smith at shortstop is a man on stage, an artist, a virtuoso, prepared at all times to break into an impromptu display of exceptional baseball choreography and giving unrehearsed performances of dazzling wit and genius bringing a glistening icing to rituals performed for over one hundred years.

Every age presents its acclaimed shortstops. There is no doubting the magical glovework demonstrated by Wagner, Marion, Aparicio and their handful of peers; but with Smith the acclaim grew to fortissimo. He simply did things that even the most venerable observers said they had never seen done before and never expected to see done again—until Smith next took the field. Like Babe Ruth at bat or Willie Mays in center field, Smith at shortstop set standards, a man taking the artistry of his profession to a higher dimension.

Elegantly named Osborne Earl, Smith was born in Mobile, Alabama, on December 26, 1954. When he was six years old, the family moved to Los Angeles, settling in the south central part of the city known as Watts, a primarily black ghetto simmering with underlying currents of resentment.

As a youngster, Smith played baseball "almost every day of the year," he wrote in his autobiography *Wizard* (written with the talented St. Louis sportswriter Rob Rains). The exception in his routine came during two weeks in the summer of 1965. Pent-up racial tensions boiled over into the Watts riots, and the National Guard were brought into the area. For those two weeks, Smith wrote, there was no baseball; there was only coming home from school and spending the night in a

locked house, where the family slept on the floor because of the danger of flying bullets.

For young Smith, baseball's future "Wizard of Oz," the way out of the ghetto was through baseball. With his unique skills shaping and dictating his future, the boy worked tirelessly and enthusiastically at cultivating them. By the hour, he would fire a rubber ball against a tier of concrete steps, moving in closer and closer, forcing himself to react more and more quickly to the rebounding ball.

Smith could not remember the first time he played shortstop; it just seemed "as if I was always there," in the only position he ever wanted to play. When he was on the field, he said later, "you probably see me at my happiest and most peaceful moments." When he was out there, he was "away," in his "own world. I can do things I want to do." (Only a player as sublimely gifted as Smith would equate that kind of inner serenity with the tensions and pressures of big-league baseball.)

Ozzie played on the baseball team at Locke High School in Los Angeles (one of his teammates was Eddie Murray), then went to California Polytechnic State University at San Luis Obispo on a partial athletic scholarship (it was here that he taught himself to switch-hit). After completing his senior year, he was selected by the San Diego Padres in the fourth round of the June 1977 free-agent draft.

There is something almost immediately radiant about a gifted young shortstop. Reviewing the careers of Joe Cronin, Arky Vaughan, Luke Appling, Lou Boudreau, Travis Jackson, Robin Yount, and others, one sees that it appears these players spent a year or two, at most, in the minor leagues, even in eras when a player's minor-league tenure could last five or six years. Smith followed this pattern, playing just the 1977 season in the minors, for Walla Walla, Washington, in the Northwest League. Since the Northwest was a rookie league, not getting underway until June, Ozzie had only 68

● *Ozzie Smith with the San Diego Padres, for whom he played for four years.*
National Baseball Library, Cooperstown, NY.

games of pro ball behind him when he made the huge leap to the major leagues the following year.

Ozzie attributes his jump from rookie ball to the majors largely to the support and encouragement of San Diego manager Alvin Dark, a top shortstop of the 1940s and 1950s. Dark worked with Ozzie in the instructional league and then in spring training in 1978. Even after the Padres made the bizarre move of firing their manager in spring training, Smith remained at short.

● *Shortstop was the only position he ever wanted to play.*

Ozzie hadn't been in the big leagues for more than a week when he made one of those defensive plays that would become his personal and inimitable signature for years to come. The Padres were playing the Atlanta Braves at home. Jeff Burroughs was the batter. He hit a ball through the box that seemed to be speeding on its way to center field for a hit. But a new force had been set loose upon the playing grounds of the National League. Smith broke to his left and dove behind second base. As he was in midair, the ball suddenly took an erratic hop and spun to Ozzie's right. He shot out his bare hand and nabbed the ball just as he was bellywhopping to the ground. He bounced right up ("He's like a damned rubber ball," one player was to grouse later) and gunned out Burroughs at first.

"That one play put me in the spotlight," Ozzie said. It was shown and re-shown on television all over the country, with many people describing it as the greatest play they had ever seen.

On September 26, 1980, in his third big-league year, Smith broke Glenn Wright's long-standing major-league record (set in 1924) for assists in a season by a shortstop. It was Smith's 602nd assist, and he ended with a total of 621. In 1980 he won his first Gold Glove, an award he especially prized because it was voted by the league's opposing managers and coaches. After that, the distinction became so routinely his— he won it every year in the 1980s—that it might well have been called "The Ozzie Smith Award."

Despite being labeled "untouchable" by Padres management, Ozzie found himself the subject of trade rumors after the 1981 season. He had been coveted by St. Louis Cardinals manager Whitey Herzog. The trade, a surprise to everyone, was announced on February 11, 1982. Ozzie Smith went to the Cardinals for shortstop Garry Templeton.

It was under Herzog that Smith began improving his hitting. After a .258 rookie year, his averages had declined to .211, .230, and .222. Ozzie's problem had been overswinging, hitting too many balls into the air, a fruitless exercise for a man of little power. Herzog told him to concentrate on hitting the ball on the ground and came up with what Ozzie described as a "fun deal." For every ball Ozzie hit into the air, he owed Herzog a buck, and for every ball Ozzie hit on the ground, Herzog owed him a buck. By the end of the year, Smith had made around $300; but more importantly, he improved his average 26 points, to .248.

With Ozzie performing his acrobatic feats at shortstop all season, the Cardinals took their first pennant in 14 years. They went on to sweep Atlanta in the playoffs and then won the World Series in a seven-game victory over the Milwaukee Brewers.

● *Whitey Herzog.*

After the 1982 season, Smith signed a three-year contract for $1 million a year (then a considerable baseball salary). His agent Ed Gottlieb said, "Ozzie commenced the era of the glove in much the same way Babe Ruth commenced the era of the home run and Sandy Koufax commenced the era of pitching." There was, of course, more than a touch of hyperbole in the statement, but the contract did give Ozzie the full recognition he had earned. Specifically, the contract underlined the fact that the Cardinals, in a home park (Busch Stadium) with dimensions favoring the pitcher, had built their club around pitching, speed, and defense, and in the context of this tactical alignment, Ozzie was a superstar.

According to Herzog, Ozzie "took two hits or a run away from our opponents every game last year. That's just as important as a guy who drives in runs."

Ozzie's next contract was signed after the 1985 season, when he helped the Cardinals to another pennant. This time the multi-year pact called for $2 million a year, and the Cardinals, in Herzog's words, "got ripped up and down baseball for paying that much money to a glove man." But this was no ordinary glove man; this was an extraordinary glove man, one without equal at his position in the history of baseball. No shortstop since Wagner had by such unanimous acclaim dominated the position. Herzog, having pronounced Ozzie superior to the greatest defensive shortstops he had ever seen (he enumerated Marion, Belanger, and Aparicio) also called him "a first-rate human being, a leader in the best sense of the word." The skipper knew that without "The Wizard" at short, the pennants of '82 and '85 would have flown elsewhere.

In 1985, Ozzie gave the Cardinals a contribution from home plate. He had known all the elation and exhilaration of splendor in the field, but in 1985, he experienced the most dramatically satisfying of all baseball thrills—thunder at home plate.

Through Ozzie Smith, baseball once again demonstrated that it was a game of the unexpected. The occasion was Game 5 of the 1985 playoffs, the Cardinals versus the Los Angeles Dodgers. The series was balanced at two apiece, and this pivotal fifth contest was tied at 2–2 when Ozzie came to bat with one out and the bases empty in the bottom of the ninth. The pitcher was right-hander Tom Niedenfuer, pitching under great pressure but with at least one assurance going for him: Ozzie was not the man to send one deep (just 13 career home runs in eight big-league seasons) and, in fact, had never in his professional career homered from the left side of the plate. Until then.

Niedenfuer fired, and Ozzie, who routinely did the impossible in the field, suddenly uncorked the improbable at home plate, by lining one just over the wall in right field, for a game-winning home run, putting the Cardinals at the brink of the pennant. They clinched the title the

● *The infield of the 1985 pennant-winning St. Louis Cardinals. Left to right, third baseman Terry Pendleton, shortstop Ozzie Smith, second baseman Tommy Herr, and first baseman Jack Clark.*

next day. Of all of baseball's theatrical home runs, Ozzie's was, statistically at least, the most unlikely. (As if to underscore this, he went homerless for the next two seasons.)

In helping the Cardinals to another pennant in 1987, Ozzie had what was arguably his finest season. In addition to his defensive work—just ten errors and a sixth fielding title with a .987 average—he batted a career-high .307 and probably should have won the Most Valuable Player Award (it went to Chicago's Andre Dawson, who dazzled the voters with 49 home runs).

Smith has proven to be one of the most durable of shortstops. Through 1990, in 9 out of 13 years, he played over 150 games a season. This has enabled him to set an array of major-league records for his position: most assists in a season (621), most years leading in assists (8), most years with 500 or more assists (8), most years leading in chances accepted (8), and the National League record for most years leading in fielding average (6). Those are the facts, plain and undeniable. It was how Ozzie Smith achieved those standards that had to be seen to be believed.

● *"The Wizard of Oz."*

● *Ozzie in 1989.*

Cal Ripkin, Jr.

CAL RIPKIN, JR.

No matter what else he achieved on the diamond—and his achievements are considerable—the veritable theme of Cal Ripkin, Jr.'s career was his consecutive game playing streak. After the 1990 season, he reached 1,411 games, the second longest streak in baseball history. Only Lou Gehrig surpassed him with 2,130. Gehrig's record had been long regarded as not only unbreakable, but unchallengeable. However, some people began computing that Ripkin could break Gehrig's record midway through the 1995 season, barring illness, injury, or a dramatic deterioration of skills.

By itself, a consecutive game playing streak is a passive and unstirring achievement, for you are only doing the very least that is expected of you: showing up and being ready to play. What made Ripkin's streak more and more noticeable and interesting was the Gehrig factor; the Oriole star was tracking an endurance record established by one of the game's supreme players and probably its most touching tragedy. Gehrig the man had always seemed stoic and remote, and with the passage of time, his record had taken on an aura of inviolability. Pointing up Gehrig's

heroic fidelity in cold statistical terms, since his enforced retirement, no one had been able to come within 900 games of his record, until Ripkin began piling up one slate after another of full-season play.

Ripkin's streak also intrigued people because it was being amassed by a shortstop, a position most vulnerable to injury. Actually, however, of the six men in baseball history with 1,000 or more consecutive games played, three have been shortstops—Everett Scott (whose 1,307 in a row was the record Gehrig broke), Joe Sewell (1,103), and Ripkin.

If shortstops are not supposed to be indestructible, neither are they supposed to be 6'4" and over 200 pounds. Ripkin is probably the biggest man ever to play shortstop in the big leagues. He is certainly the most physically formidable ever to star at the position.

Ripkin was a baseball brat from the very beginning. When he was born, on August 24, 1960, at Havre de Grace, Maryland, his father, Calvin

Edwin, Sr., was a twenty-four-year-old catcher with Baltimore's Fox Cities farm team in the Three-Eye League. The Ripkins and Baltimore have been entwined ever since Cal, Sr., first joined the organization in 1957. While he never broke the surface of major-league ball as a player, Cal, Sr., made it as a coach, then manager, and then coach again (after managing in Baltimore's minor-league system for 14 years).

Every June, Cal, his siblings (including younger brother Billy, his future double-play partner with the Orioles), and his mother would pack up and follow the career trail of Cal, Sr. The stops included Leesburg, Florida; Fox Cities, Illinois; Aberdeen, Washington; Miami, Florida; Elmira, New York; Asheville, North Carolina; Rochester, New York; and Dallas-Fort Worth, Texas. For young Cal it was a geography lesson and a baseball education. Not only did he learn the game by watching it at increasingly sophisticated levels and associating with professional players, but he gained an invaluable poise and professionalism. If he was one of the most intuitively intelligent of players from the moment he reached the major leagues at the age of twenty-one in 1981, it was due, in part, to the long and intimate apprenticeship he had served.

"He wasn't just a talented kid with a few years of minor-league experience when he joined the Orioles," one Baltimore scout said. "He was what you might describe as a highly educated player. He understood the game and had mastered all the fundamentals. Right from the beginning he began studying the opposing hitters as well as his own pitchers, learning how to position himself. Some shortstops never fully learn that, depending on their own quickness to get to balls. But Cal soon became a master at positioning himself; added to his natural abilities, it eventually made him almost airtight out there."

That Ripkin would be a professional baseball player was inevitable. He had the talent, the desire, and encouragement from his parents. That he would sign with the Orioles was a foregone conclusion.

● *"A baseball brat from the very beginning."*

In the second round of the free-agent draft in June 1978, Baltimore selected Ripkin as an infielder-pitcher. In fact, most major league teams had scouted him as a pitcher.

"If he had come up as a pitcher," said Joe Altobelli, who managed the Orioles for several years, "he'd probably be winning 15 to 20 games a year by now. He's just that kind of athlete, capable of excelling at anything he does."

Ripkin began his professional career with the Bluefield, Virginia, club in the Appalachian League. He got into 63 games—all at shortstop, batted .264, hit no home runs, and led the league in errors with 33.

In 1979 he was with Miami in the Florida State League, dividing his time between short and third and batting .303. At this point, the Orioles felt his height would prove a defensive liability at shortstop. So in 1980 he was a third

● *Baltimore manager Earl Weaver, who switched Ripkin from third base to shortstop.*

baseman for Charlotte in the Southern League, and a year later, he was still posted at the bag with Rochester in the International League.

In the spring of 1982 Ripkin made the Orioles as a third baseman. On July 1, however, manager Earl Weaver switched Ripkin to shortstop, believing the rookie star could handle the more demanding and important (as well as the harder to fill) position. Those who didn't think Cal possessed the range for the job were soon dissuaded.

"I don't see too many balls that get through him," Robin Yount said. "He's got great hands. And it seems like he's always in the right place."

"He's surprised me," said Alan Trammell. "I thought he was too big to play shortstop, but he's played a helluva game there."

It was Baltimore reliever Tippy Martinez who paid the rookie the highest compliment when he said "He's like Belanger."

Twenty-two years old now and filling out physically, Ripkin also gave the Orioles more than they expected at home plate: 28 home runs, 93 runs batted in, and a .264 batting average. His all-around play earned him the American League's Rookie of the Year Award.

A year later, in 1983, Cal Ripkin, Jr., soared to stardom. Putting together a season of spectacular success, he helped lead the Orioles to the Eastern Division title, a playoff victory over the Chicago White Sox, and a World Series victory over the Philadelphia Phillies. He batted .318, hit 27 home runs, drove in 102 runs, and had league-leading figures in doubles (47), hits (211), runs scored (121), and at bats (663), in addition to leading shortstops with 534 assists. He also played every inning of every game, which he continued to do until 1983, when Cal, Sr., took over the team and induced his son to take off a few innings now and then.

After the season, Ripkin was voted the American League's Most Valuable Player, crowning two of the most successful rookie and sophomore seasons any player has ever enjoyed: Rookie of the Year, world championship, MVP Award.

Ripkin followed his outstanding 1983 season with a .304 average in 1984 and maintained his remarkable consistency at bat and in the field where, he was becoming ever more skilled at solving the geometry of playing shortstop.

He seemed to thrive on the tolls and toils of his position, playing through ankle sprains, aching muscles, sore elbows, colds, and viruses; making diving stops; and being bowled over by baserunners, but always getting up, coming back, building an image of indestructibility that began to draw more and more attention. Perhaps too much attention.

● *Ripkin out where he makes few mistakes.*

● *Detroit's Eddie Brinkman. In 1990, Ripkin broke his 1972 record for consecutive errorless games.*

The consecutive game playing streak soon became the first thing mentioned when Ripkin's name came up. Overlooked was the fact that he had become the American League's perennial starter on its All-Star team and that, by the late 1980s, he was approaching a home-run record for shortstops. Whenever he went into a slump the streak was blamed: "He's worn out."

But Ripkin put his endurance record into perspective: "People talk as though the streak was one continual block of games. But it isn't. You play 162 straight games and then you have five months off."

In 1984, Ripkin set an American League record for shortstops with 583 assists; it was one of the five times he led in the 1980s. Leading in putouts four times enabled him to tie the league record.

In 1990 Ripkin began drawing attention with another kind of streak—consecutive errorless games. The American League record of 72 had been established by Detroit's Eddie Brinkman in 1972. Ripkin charged at the record, ate it whole and kept going. His next target was the major league mark of 88, set by the New York Mets' Kevin Elster in 1988–89. On July 19, 1990, Cal tied the record and maintained a steady, inerrant course, compiling a remarkable 95 straight errorless games before finally mishandling a ground ball in Kansas City on July 28. During the streak he handled 431 straight chances impeccably, breaking the old mark for a season by exactly 100. It was an astonishing margin by which to set a new record.

● *The Ripkins of Baltimore. Left to right, Billy, Cal Sr., and Cal Jr.*

At the end of the season, Ripkin's defensive ledger was one of very few blots: just three errors and a .996 fielding average. With both of these new standards, shortstops of the future will be hard pressed to do better. The previous record low for errors was Brinkman's seven in 1972, and the previous best fielding average for 150 or more games was Brinkman's, again in 1972, and Ripkin's own .990 in 1989 (a year in which Ripkin committed just eight errors).

Another defensive mark set in 1990 was of special pride to the Ripkin family. Younger brother Billy, now at second base for Baltimore, and Cal, Jr., combined for the lowest errors total (11) by a shortstop-second baseman combination in major-league history.

Ripkin augmented his near-flawless fielding with 21 home runs and 84 RBIs, giving him nine straight years of over 20 homers and 80 RBIs. At the end of the season he had a career total of 225 home runs, enabling him to surpass Vern Stephens' old American League record for shortstops of 213.

Cal Ripkin, Sr., managed the Orioles in 1987 and for a few games in 1988. He was then replaced by Frank Robinson. Cal, Sr., later returned to the club as a coach, and so the Ripkins went into the 1990s as a unit: Cal, Sr., on the coaching lines; Cal, Jr., at shortstop; and Billy at second base. Recalling Cal, Jr., as a youngster, Cal, Sr., said, "He always wanted to be a ballplayer. It was his own idea. He just liked to play." And play. And play.

AND NOT FORGETTING ...

Bobby Wallace

Before the ascendancy of Honus Wagner in the early years of the twentieth century, the man generally acclaimed baseball's premier shortstop was Roderick (Bobby) Wallace, a big leaguer for all or parts of 25 seasons (1894–1918). Wallace began his career as a pitcher for Cleveland, then in the National League, moving to third base in 1897. In 1899 he switched to shortstop, where he starred for St. Louis in the National League and then St. Louis in the American League. A .267 lifetime hitter, Wallace was noted for his fielding. He was elected to the Hall of Fame in 1953, the first American League shortstop to be so honored.

Joe Tinker

Front man on baseball's most famous double-play combination, Joe Tinker played from 1902 to 1913, then jumped to the Federal League for two years. He spent the first 11 of his big-league seasons with the Chicago Cubs. A .263 lifetime hitter, Tinker was considered an outstanding defensive shortstop in an era of floppy gloves and camel-backed infields. He led in fielding five times.

Dave Bancroft

The switch-hitting Dave Bancroft came to the big leagues with the Philadelphia Phillies in 1915, just in time to help the club to its first pennant. He was traded to the New York Giants in 1920 and helped that club to the World Series in each of the next three years. Bancroft was known as a brainy shortstop, quick-handed and far-ranging. He led in putouts four times and assists three times. He later played for the Boston Braves and Brooklyn Dodgers, retiring in 1930 with a .279 career average. He made the Hall of Fame in 1971.

Everett Scott

Everett Scott played in the big leagues from 1914 through 1926, primarily for the Boston Red Sox and New York Yankees. He is co-holder (with Luis Aparicio) of one of baseball's most impressive defensive records, leading American League shortstops in fielding average for eight consecutive seasons (1916–1923). A .249 lifetime hitter, Scott was a durable player—it was his record of 1,307 consecutive games that Lou Gehrig broke on his way to playing 2,130 games in a row.

Joe Sewell

Joe Sewell possesses one of baseball's most enviable distinctions: he was the toughest man to strike out. In 7,132 official times at bat, he fanned just 114 times. Sewell played shortstop for Cleveland from 1920 through 1928, when he switched to third base. As a shortstop he led four times each in putouts and assists and twice in fielding. He played his last three years with the Yankees, retiring in 1933. His uncanny batting eye earned him a .312 career average. He was elected to the Hall of Fame in 1977.

Dick Bartell

They called him "Rowdy Richard" for his fiery style of play, which he displayed on big-league infields from 1927 through 1943. Bartell's heyday years were with the Pittsburgh Pirates, the Philadelphia Phillies, and New York Giants. Later he played for the Detroit Tigers and Chicago Cubs. Six times a .300 hitter, he had a lifetime mark of .284. Bartell played 1,702 games at shortstop, leading four times in putouts and three times in assists.

Billy Jurges

The sparkplug shortstop in the Chicago Cubs' pennant winners in 1932, 1935, and 1938, Billy Jurges was one of the fine fielding players of his era. His career, divided between the Cubs and New York Giants, ran from 1931 through 1947. A .258 lifetime hitter, Jurges led in fielding five times (which is one under the league record).

Phil Rizzuto

The man at shortstop for nine New York Yankee pennant winners was Phil Rizzuto. He was voted the American League's Most Valuable Player in 1950, when he batted .324. Extraordinarily quick and sure-handed in the field, Rizzuto once held the American League record for consecutive errorless chances by a shortstop, with 289, and twice led in fielding. He played from 1941 to 1956, with three years out for military service. His lifetime batting average was .273.

Vern Stephens

Noted more for his hitting than his fielding, Vern Stephens nevertheless led American League shortstops three times in assists and once in fielding. He was a premier long-baller, leading once in home runs and three times in runs batted in, with a colossal high of 159 runs batted in during 1949, followed by 144 a year later. Stephens' best years were spent with the St. Louis Browns and Boston Red Sox. He also played for the Chicago White Sox and Baltimore Orioles. He batted .286 for his career, which ran from 1941 to 1955.

Alvin Dark

Rookie of the Year with the Boston Braves in 1948, Alvin Dark was a shortstop who was noted for making the "clutch play." Four times a .300 hitter (.289 lifetime), Dark played for the Braves,

New York Giants, St. Louis Cardinals, Chicago Cubs, Philadelphia Phillies, and Milwaukee Braves in a career that ran from 1947 to 1960. A star on three pennant winners, Dark led National League shortstops three times in putouts and once in assists.

Dick Groat

Dick Groat was the National League's Most Valuable Player in 1960, as well as the batting champion (.325). He never played in the minor leagues but came to the majors with Pittsburgh in 1952. After two years in the military, he became a regular shortstop with the Pirates (for whom he was MVP), St. Louis Cardinals, and Philadelphia Phillies until 1966. He retired in 1967 with the San Francisco Giants. Despite being somewhat error-prone (he led six times), Groat led shortstops four times in putouts and twice in assists. His lifetime batting average was .286.

Roy McMillan

Despite a lightweight bat (.243 lifetime average), Roy McMillan played 2,028 games at shortstop (seventh on the list among twentieth-century shortstops), a tribute to his dazzling glovework. He played most of his career with the Cincinnati Reds before being traded to the Milwaukee Braves and then finished up with the New York Mets. His career ran from 1951 to 1966. McMillan's superb defensive work enabled him to lead three times in putouts, five times in assists, and four times in fielding average.

Maury Wills

It was Maury Wills who re-introduced the stolen base as an offensive weapon with his landmark 104 steals in 1962. That year he helped the Los Angeles Dodgers to the pennant and won the

Most Valuable Player Award. Wills, who led in stolen bases six times, was a hard-working, highly disciplined player who made himself a major-league star. A .281 career hitter, he played from 1959 to 1972 with the Dodgers, Pittsburgh Pirates, and Montreal Expos.

Mark Belanger

Young shortstops coming into the American League in the 1970s were all told the same thing: "Watch Belanger; that's how it's done." Belanger played with the Baltimore Orioles from 1965 through 1981, finishing with the Los Angeles Dodgers a year later. Despite a weak bat (.228 lifetime), he played 1,942 big-league games at shortstop. Incomparable in all facets of defensive play, he holds the American League record (through 1989) for the highest career fielding average for shortstops in 1,000 or more games (.977).

Bert Campaneris

Some people thought the most valuable player on the Oakland Athletic teams that won three straight world championships and five straight division titles in the 1970s was shortstop Bert Campaneris. Campaneris played 2,097 games at short, sixth highest total for a twentieth-century player. A .259 lifetime hitter, he was a basepath speedster, leading in stolen bases six times. He played from 1964 to 1983 with the Kansas City and Oakland Athletics, Texas Rangers, California Angels, and New York Yankees.

Larry Bowa

The man who holds the major-league record for the highest lifetime fielding average for a shortstop, in 1,000 or more games, is Larry Bowa, with a .980 mark. He also holds the National League records for highest fielding average for 150 or more games (.987, which he achieved twice, in 1971 and 1972) and for 100 or more games (.991, which he rang up in 146 games in 1979). A .260 career hitter, Bowa played from 1970 through 1985, spending the bulk of his career with the Philadelphia Phillies, and finishing up with the Chicago Cubs and New York Mets. He led the league in fielding six times, a record he shares with Ozzie Smith (through the 1989 season), and his 2,222 games at shortstop stand as the all-time National League high for the position.

Tony Fernandez

After completing six full seasons in the major leagues in 1990, Toronto's Tony Fernandez had earned a reputation as one of the game's stellar young shortstops. Twice a .300 hitter, his 213 hits in 1986 are the most ever accumulated by a shortstop in a single season. His .992 fielding average in 1989 set a record for shortstops (broken by Cal Ripkin a year later). There seems little question that future editions of this book will find Fernandez where many believe he already belongs—on the front list.

LIFETIME RECORDS

Statistics courtesy of *The Sporting News*

Honus Wagner

Year Club	League	Pos.	G.	AB.	R.	H.	2B.	3B.	HR.	RBI.	B.A.	PO.	A.	E.	F.A.
1895—Steubenville	Int. St.	SS	44	....	....	....	....	....	....	....	.402	....	....	....	....
1895—Mansfield	Ohio St.						(No records available)								
1895—Adrian	Mich. St.	S-O	20	....	....	....	....	....	....	....	.365	....	....	....	....
1895—Warren	Iron-Oil	SS	65	....	....	....	....	....	....	....	.369	....	....	....	....
1896—Paterson	Atl.	1-3-OF	109	416	106	145	....	....	....	....	.349	802	79	41	.956
1897—Paterson	Atlantic	3B	74	301	61	114	....	....	....	....	.379	104	107	24	.898
1897—Louisville	Nat.	OF	61	241	38	83	17	4	2	....	.344	105	17	11	.917
1898—Louisville	Nat.	1B-3B	148	591	80	180	31	4	10	....	.305	827	165	32	.969
1899—Louisville(a)	Nat.	3B-OF	144	549	102	197	47	13	7	....	.359	197	185	30	.927
1900—Pittsburgh	Nat.	OF	134	528	107	201	45	22	4	....	.381	177	13	6	.969
1901—Pittsburgh	Nat.	IF-OF	141	556	100	196	39	10	6	....	.353	299	279	47	.925
1902—Pittsburgh	Nat.	IF-OF	137	538	105	177	33	16	3	....	.329	526	171	34	.953
1903—Pittsburgh	Nat.	SS	129	512	97	182	30	19	5	....	.355	303	397	50	.933
1904—Pittsburgh	Nat.	SS	132	490	97	171	44	14	4	....	.349	274	367	49	.929
1905—Pittsburgh	Nat.	SS	147	548	114	199	22	14	6	....	.363	353	517	60	.935
1906—Pittsburgh	Nat.	SS	140	516	103	175	38	9	2	....	.339	334	473	51	.941
1907—Pittsburgh	Nat.	SS	142	515	98	180	38	14	6	91	.350	314	428	49	.938
1908—Pittsburgh	Nat.	SS	151	568	100	201	39	19	10	106	.354	354	469	50	.943
1909—Pittsburgh	Nat.	SS	137	495	92	168	39	10	5	102	.339	344	430	49	.940
1910—Pittsburgh	Nat.	SS	150	556	90	178	34	8	4	84	.320	337	413	52	.935
1911—Pittsburgh	Nat.	SS-1B	130	473	87	158	23	16	9	108	.334	471	321	46	.945
1912—Pittsburgh	Nat.	SS	145	558	91	181	35	20	7	94	.324	341	462	32	.962
1913—Pittsburgh	Nat.	SS	114	413	51	124	18	4	3	55	.300	289	323	24	.962
1914—Pittsburgh	Nat.	3B-SS	150	552	60	139	15	9	1	46	.252	339	457	43	.949
1915—Pittsburgh	Nat.	SS	156	566	68	155	32	17	6	78	.274	298	395	38	.948
1916—Pittsburgh	Nat.	1B-SS	123	432	45	124	15	9	1	38	.287	409	272	33	.954
1917—Pittsburgh	Nat.	1-3 SS	74	230	15	61	7	1	0	22	.265	476	74	13	.977
Major League Totals			2785	10427	1740	3430	651	252	101	....	.329	7367	6628	799	.946

WORLD SERIES RECORD

Year Club	League	Pos.	G	AB.	R.	H.	2B.	3B.	HR.	RBI.	B.A.	PO.	A.	E.	F.A.
1903—Pittsburgh	Nat.	SS	8	27	2	6	1	0	0	3	.222	13	27	6	.870
1909—Pittsburgh	Nat.	SS	7	24	4	8	2	1	0	7	.333	13	23	2	.947
World Series Totals			15	51	6	14	3	1	0	10	.275	26	50	8	.905

Rabbit Maranville

Year Club	League	Pos.	G.	AB.	R.	H.	2B.	3B.	HR.	RBI.	B.A.	PO.	A.	E.	F.A.
1911—New Bedford	N. Eng.	SS	117	422	41	96	17	9	2	....	.227	256	345	61	.908
1912—New Bedford	N. Eng.	SS	122	452	65	128	22	4	4	....	.283	268	441	42	.944
1912—Boston	Nat.	SS	26	86	8	18	2	0	0	7	.209	46	97	11	.929
1913—Boston	Nat.	SS	143	571	68	141	13	8	2	44	.247	317	475	43	.949
1914—Boston	Nat.	SS	156	586	74	144	23	6	4	72	.246	407	574	65	.938
1915—Boston	Nat.	SS	149	509	51	124	23	6	2	47	.244	391	486	55	.941
1916—Boston	Nat.	SS	155	604	79	142	16	13	4	36	.235	386	515	50	.947
1917—Boston	Nat.	SS	142	561	69	146	19	13	3	41	.260	341	474	46	.947
1918—Boston(a)	Nat.	SS	11	38	3	12	0	1	0	3	.316	34	34	5	.932
1919—Boston	Nat.	SS	131	480	44	128	18	10	5	43	.267	361	488	53	.941
1920—Boston(b)	Nat.	SS	134	493	48	131	19	15	1	43	.266	354	462	45	.948
1921—Pittsburgh	Nat.	SS	153	612	90	180	25	12	1	70	.294	325	529	34	.962
1922—Pittsburgh	Nat.	SS-2B	155	672	115	198	26	15	0	63	.295	419	512	36	.963
1923—Pittsburgh	Nat.	SS	141	581	78	161	19	9	1	41	.277	332	505	30	.965
1924—Pittsburgh(c)	Nat.	2B	152	594	62	158	33	20	2	71	.266	365	568	26	.973
1925—Chicago(d)	Nat.	SS-2B	75	266	37	62	10	3	0	23	.233	162	261	20	.955
1926—Brooklyn	Nat.	SS-2B	78	234	32	55	8	5	0	24	.235	161	246	19	.955
1927—Rochester	Int.	SS	135	507	81	151	25	10	1	63	.298	329	440	24	.970
1927—St. Louis	Nat.	SS	9	29	0	7	1	0	0	1	.241	17	34	2	.962
1928—St. Louis(e)	Nat.	SS	112	366	40	88	14	10	1	34	.240	236	362	19	.969
1929—Boston	Nat.	SS	146	560	87	159	26	10	0	55	.284	319	536	35	.961
1930—Boston	Nat.	SS	142	558	85	157	26	8	2	43	.281	343	445	29	.965
1931—Boston	Nat.	SS-2B	145	562	69	146	22	5	0	33	.260	289	453	41	.948
1932—Boston	Nat.	2B	149	571	67	134	20	4	0	37	.235	402	473	22	.975
1933—Boston	Nat.	2B	143	478	46	104	15	4	0	38	.218	362	384	22	.971
1934—Boston	Nat.						(Broke leg in spring exhibition game and did not play)								
1935—Boston	Nat.	2B	23	67	3	10	2	0	0	5	.149	32	46	3	.963
1936—Elmira	NYP	2B-SS	123	427	65	138	15	2	0	54	.323	322	319	28	.958
1939—Albany	East.	2B	6	17	3	2	0	0	0	2	.118	10	8	8	.692
Major League Totals			2670	10078	1255	2605	380	177	28	874	.258	6401	8959	711	.956

WORLD SERIES RECORD

Year Club	League	Pos.	G.	AB.	R.	H.	2B.	3B.	HR.	RBI.	B.A.	PO.	A.	E.	F.A.
1914—Boston	Nat.	SS	4	13	1	4	0	0	0	3	.308	7	13	1	.952
1928—St. Louis	Nat.	SS	4	13	2	4	1	0	0	0	.308	11	3	1	.933
World Series Totals			8	26	3	8	1	0	0	3	.308	18	16	2	.944

Travis Jackson

Year Club	League	Pos.	G.	AB.	R.	H.	2B.	3B.	HR.	RBI.	B.A.	PO.	A.	E.	F.A.
1921—Little Rock	South.	SS	39	130	11	26	5	0	1	12	.200	65	96	21	.885
1922—Little Rock	South.	SS	147	521	59	146	18	9	7	....	.280	279	455	73	.910
1922—New York	Nat.	SS	3	8	1	0	0	0	0	0	.000	3	7	1	.909
1923—New York	Nat.	3B-SS	96	327	45	90	12	7	4	37	.275	107	265	23	.942
1924—New York	Nat.	SS	151	596	81	180	26	8	11	76	.302	332	534	58	.937
1925—New York	Nat.	SS	112	411	51	117	15	2	9	59	.285	277	366	40	.941
1926—New York	Nat.	SS	111	385	64	126	24	8	8	51	.327	256	351	24	.962
1927—New York	Nat.	SS	127	469	67	149	29	4	14	98	.318	287	444	37	.952
1928—New York	Nat.	SS	150	537	73	145	35	6	14	77	.270	354	547	45	.952
1929—New York	Nat.	SS	149	551	92	162	21	12	21	94	.294	329	552	28	.969
1930—New York	Nat.	SS	116	431	70	146	27	8	13	82	.339	218	441	30	.956
1931—New York	Nat.	SS	145	555	65	172	26	10	5	71	.310	303	496	25	.970
1932—New York	Nat.	SS	52	195	23	50	17	1	4	38	.256	106	166	22	.925
1933—New York	Nat.	3B-SS	53	122	11	30	5	0	0	12	.246	52	87	11	.927
1934—New York	Nat.	3B-SS	137	523	75	140	26	7	16	101	.268	292	477	43	.947
1935—New York	Nat.	3B	128	511	74	154	20	12	9	80	.301	139	220	20	.947
1936—New York	Nat.	3B	126	465	41	107	8	1	7	53	.230	99	196	15	.952
1937—Jersey City	Int.	SS	6	20	0	5	0	0	0	1	.250	11	17	2	.933
1938—Jersey City	Int.	3B-SS	10	17	0	5	1	0	0	2	.294	3	7	0	1.000
Major League Totals—15 Years			1656	6086	833	1768	291	86	135	929	.291	3154	5149	422	.952

WORLD SERIES RECORD

Year Club	League	Pos.	G.	AB.	R.	H.	2B.	3B.	HR.	RBI.	B.A.	PO.	A.	E.	F.A.
1923—New York	Nat.	PH	1	1	0	0	0	0	0	0	.000	0	0	0	.000
1924—New York	Nat.	SS	7	27	3	2	0	0	0	1	.074	8	20	3	.903
1933—New York	Nat.	3B	5	18	3	4	1	0	0	2	.222	3	16	1	.950
1936—New York	Nat.	3B	6	21	1	4	0	0	0	1	.190	2	8	3	.769
World Series Totals—4 Years			19	67	7	10	1	0	0	4	.149	13	44	7	.891

Joe Cronin

Year Club	League	Pos.	G.	AB.	R.	H.	2B.	3B.	HR.	RBI.	B.A.	PO.	A.	E.	F.A.
1925—Johnstown	Mid.-Atl.	2B-SS	99	352	64	110	18	11	3	....	.313	....	....	....	....
1926—Pittsburgh	Nat.	2B-SS	38	83	9	22	2	2	0	11	.265	55	82	3	.979
1926—New Haven	East.	SS	66	244	61	78	11	8	2	....	.320	136	222	27	.930
1927—Pittsburgh	Nat.	SS	12	22	2	5	1	0	0	3	.227	12	10	4	.846
1928—Kansas City	A.A.	SS	74	241	34	59	10	6	2	32	.245	87	146	14	.943
1928—Washington	Amer.	SS	63	227	23	55	10	4	0	25	.242	133	190	16	.953
1929—Washington	Amer.	SS	145	494	72	139	29	8	8	60	.281	285	459	62	.923
1930—Washington	Amer.	SS	154	587	127	203	42	9	13	126	.346	336	509	35	.960
1931—Washington	Amer.	SS	156	611	103	187	44	13	12	126	.306	323	488	43	.950
1932—Washington	Amer.	SS	143	557	95	177	43	18	6	116	.318	306	448	32	.959
1933—Washington	Amer.	SS	152	602	89	186	45	11	5	118	.309	297	528	34	.960
1934—Washington(a)	Amer.	SS	127	504	68	143	30	9	7	101	.284	246	486	38	.951
1935—Boston	Amer.	1B-SS	144	556	70	164	37	14	9	95	.295	277	435	37	.951
1936—Boston	Amer.	SS-3B	81	295	36	83	22	4	2	43	.281	133	229	26	.933
1937—Boston	Amer.	SS	148	570	102	175	40	4	18	110	.307	300	414	31	.958
1938—Boston	Amer.	SS	143	530	98	172	51	5	17	94	.325	304	449	36	.954
1939—Boston	Amer.	SS	143	520	97	160	33	3	19	107	.308	306	437	32	.959
1940—Boston	Amer.	SS-3B	149	548	104	156	35	6	24	111	.285	253	445	38	.948
1941—Boston	Amer.	1-SS-3-OF	143	518	98	161	38	8	6	95	.311	247	362	27	.958
1942—Boston	Amer.	1B-SS-3B	45	79	7	24	3	0	4	24	.304	47	28	6	.926
1943—Boston	Amer.	3B	59	77	8	24	4	0	5	29	.312	12	18	1	.968
1944—Boston	Amer.	1B	76	191	24	46	7	0	5	28	.241	428	27	9	.981
1945—Boston(b)	Amer.	3B	3	8	1	3	0	0	0	1	.375	2	8	0	1.000
American League Totals			2074	7474	1222	2258	513	116	170	1409	.302	4235	5960	503	.953
National League Totals			50	105	11	27	3	2	0	14	.257	67	92	7	.958
Major League Totals			2124	7579	1233	2285	5516	118	170	1423	.301	4302	6052	510	.953

WORLD SERIES RECORD

Year Club	League	Pos.	G.	AB.	R.	H.	2B.	3B.	HR.	RBI.	B.A.	PO.	A.	E.	F.A.
1933—Washington	Amer.	SS	5	22	1	7	0	0	0	2	.318	7	15	1	.957

Luke Appling

Year Club	League	Pos.	G.	AB.	R.	H.	2B.	3B.	HR.	RBI.	B.A.	PO.	A.	E.	F.A.
1930—Atlanta	South.	SS	104	374	63	122	19	17	5	75	.326	224	302	42	.926
1930—Chicago	Amer.	SS	6	26	2	8	2	0	0	2	.308	12	17	4	.879
1931—Chicago	Amer.	SS-2B	96	297	36	69	13	4	1	28	.232	151	233	43	.899
1932—Chicago	Amer.	INF	139	489	66	134	20	10	3	63	.274	270	419	49	.934
1933—Chicago	Amer.	SS	151	612	90	197	36	10	6	85	.322	314	534	55	.939
1934—Chicago	Amer.	SS-2B	118	452	75	137	28	6	2	61	.303	264	357	35	.947
1935—Chicago	Amer.	SS	153	525	94	161	28	6	1	71	.307	335	556	39	.958
1936—Chicago	Amer.	SS	138	526	111	204	31	7	6	128	.388	320	471	41	.951
1937—Chicago	Amer.	SS	154	574	98	182	42	8	4	77	.317	280	541	49	.944
1938—Chicago(a)	Amer.	SS	81	294	41	89	14	0	0	44	.303	149	258	20	.953
1939—Chicago	Amer.	SS	148	516	82	162	16	6	0	56	.314	289	461	39	.951
1940—Chicago	Amer.	SS	150	566	96	197	27	13	0	79	.348	307	436	37	.953
1941—Chicago	Amer.	SS	154	592	93	186	26	8	1	57	.314	294	473	42	.948
1942—Chicago	Amer.	SS	142	543	78	142	26	4	3	53	.262	269	418	38	.948
1943—Chicago	Amer.	SS	155	585	63	192	33	2	3	80	.328	300	500	36	.957
1944—							(In Military Service)								
1945—Chicago(b)	Amer.	SS	18	57	12	21	2	2	1	10	.368	37	56	7	.930
1946—Chicago	Amer.	SS	149	582	59	180	27	5	1	55	.309	252	505	39	.951
1947—Chicago	Amer.	SS-3B	139	503	67	154	29	0	8	49	.306	233	423	35	.949
1948—Chicago	Amer.	3B-SS	139	497	63	156	16	2	0	47	.314	217	373	35	.944
1949—Chicago	Amer.	SS	142	492	82	148	21	5	5	58	.301	253	450	26	.964
1950—Chicago	Amer.	INF	50	128	11	30	3	4	0	13	.234	128	62	3	.984
Major League Totals			2422	8856	1319	2749	440	102	45	1116	.310	4674	7543	672	.948

Arky Vaughan

Year Club	League	Pos.	G.	AB.	R.	H.	2B.	3B.	HR.	RBI.	B.A.	PO.	A.	E.	P.A.
1931—Wichita	West.	SS-3B	132	494	145	167	21	16	21	81	.338	216	352	32	.947
1932—Pittsburgh	Nat.	SS	129	497	71	158	15	10	4	61	.318	247	403	46	.934
1933—Pittsburgh	Nat.	SS	152	573	85	180	29	19	9	97	.314	310	487	46	.945
1934—Pittsburgh	Nat.	SS	149	558	115	186	41	11	12	94	.333	329	480	41	.952
1935—Pittsburgh	Nat.	SS	137	499	108	192	34	10	19	99	.385	249	422	35	.950
1936—Pittsburgh	Nat.	SS	156	568	122	190	30	11	9	78	.335	327	477	47	.945
1937—Pittsburgh	Nat.	SS-OF	126	469	71	151	17	17	5	72	.322	257	335	27	.956
1938—Pittsburgh	Nat.	SS	148	541	88	174	35	5	7	68	.322	306	507	33	.961
1939—Pittsburgh	Nat.	SS	152	595	94	182	30	11	6	62	.306	330	531	34	.962
1940—Pittsburgh	Nat.	SS-3B	156	594	113	178	40	15	7	95	.300	309	546	52	.943
1941—Pittsburgh(a)	Nat.	SS-3B	106	374	69	118	20	7	6	38	.316	174	298	21	.957
1942—Brooklyn	Nat.	3-2B-SS	128	495	82	137	18	4	2	49	.277	130	225	14	.962
1943—Brooklyn	Nat.	3B-SS	149	610	112	186	39	6	5	66	.305	237	375	21	.967
1944-45-46—Brooklyn	Nat.						(Voluntarily retired)									
1947—Brooklyn	Nat.	3B-OF	64	126	24	41	5	2	2	25	.325	56	20	0	1.000
1948—Brooklyn	Nat.	3B-OF	65	123	19	30	3	0	3	22	.244	47	14	0	1.000
1949—San Francisco	P.C.L.	OF	97	281	50	81	10	6	2	26	.288	129	4	2	.985
Major League Totals			1817	6622	1173	2103	356	128	96	926	.318	3308	5120	417	.953

WORLD SERIES RECORD

Year Club	League	Pos.	G.	AB.	R.	H.	2B.	3B.	HR.	RBI.	B.A.	PO.	A.	E.	F.A.
1947—Brooklyn	Nat.	PH	3	2	0	1	1	0	0	0	.500	0	0	0	.000

Lou Boudreau

Year Club	League	Pos.	G.	AB.	R.	H.	2B.	3B.	RH.	RBI.	B.A.	PO.	A.	E.	F.A.
1938—Cedar Rapids	I.I.I.	3B	60	231	56	67	13	4	3	29	.290	74	128	14	.935
1938—Cleveland	Amer.	3B	1	1	0	0	0	0	0	0	.000	0	0	0	.000
1939—Buffalo	Int.	SS	115	481	88	159	32	7	17	57	.331	234	371	38	.941
1939—Cleveland	Amer.	SS	53	225	42	58	15	4	0	19	.258	103	184	14	.953
1940—Cleveland	Amer.	SS	155	627	97	185	46	10	9	101	.295	277	454	24	.968
1941—Cleveland	Amer.	SS	148	579	95	149	45	8	10	56	.257	296	444	26	.966
1942—Cleveland	Amer.	SS	147	506	57	143	18	10	2	58	.283	281	426	26	.965

Year Club	League	Pos.	G.	AB.	R.	H.	2B.	3B.	RH.	RBI.	B.A.	PO.	A.	E.	F.A.
1943—Cleveland	Amer.	SS-C	152	539	69	154	32	7	3	67	.286	331	489	25	.970
1944—Cleveland	Amer.	SS-C	150	584	91	191	45	5	3	67	.327	340	517	19	.978
1945—Cleveland	Amer.	SS	97	345	50	106	24	1	3	48	.307	217	289	9	.983
1946—Cleveland	Amer.	SS	140	515	51	151	30	6	6	62	.293	315	405	22	.970
1947—Cleveland	Amer.	SS	150	538	79	165	45	3	4	67	.307	305	475	14	.982
1948—Cleveland	Amer.	SS-C	152	560	116	199	34	6	18	106	.355	297	483	20	.975
1949—Cleveland	Amer.	INF	134	475	53	135	20	3	4	60	.284	253	353	12	.981
1950—Cleveland(a)	Amer.	INF	81	260	23	70	13	2	1	29	.269	156	176	4	.988
1951—Boston	Amer.	INF	82	273	37	73	18	1	5	47	.267	94	181	15	.948
1952—Boston	Amer.	SS-3B	4	2	1	0	0	0	0	2	.000	0	1	0	1.000
Major League Totals			1646	6029	861	1779	385	66	68	789	.295	3265	4877	230	.973

WORLD SERIES RECORD

Year Club	League	Pos.	G.	AB.	R.	H.	2B.	3B.	HR.	RBI.	B.A.	PO.	A.	E.	F.A.
1948—Cleveland	Amer.	SS	6	22	1	6	4	0	0	0	.273	11	14	0	1.000

Pee Wee Reese

Year Club	League	Pos.	G.	AB.	R.	H.	2B.	3B.	HR.	RBI.	B.A.	PO.	A.	E.	F.A.
1938—Louisville	A.A.	SS	138	483	68	134	21	8	3	54	.277	239	457	45	.939
1939—Louisville	A.A.	SS	149	506	78	141	22	18	4	57	.279	307	470	47	.943
1940—Brooklyn(a)	Nat.	SS	84	312	58	85	8	4	5	28	.272	190	238	18	.960
1941—Brooklyn	Nat.	SS	152	595	76	136	23	5	2	46	.229	346	473	47	.946
1942—Brooklyn	Nat.	SS	151	564	87	144	24	5	3	53	.255	337	482	35	.959
1943-44-45—Brooklyn	Nat.	SS						(In Military Service)							
1946—Brooklyn	Nat.	SS	152	542	79	154	16	10	5	60	.284	285	463	26	.966
1947—Brooklyn	Nat.	SS	142	476	81	135	24	4	12	73	.284	266	441	25	.966
1948—Brooklyn	Nat.	SS	151	566	96	155	31	4	9	75	.274	335	453	31	.962
1949—Brooklyn	Nat.	SS	155	617	132	172	27	3	16	73	.279	316	454	18	.977
1950—Brooklyn	Nat.	SS-3B	141	531	97	138	21	5	11	52	.260	291	414	26	.964
1951—Brooklyn	Nat.	SS	154	616	94	176	20	8	10	84	.286	292	422	35	.953
1952—Brooklyn	Nat.	SS	149	559	94	152	18	8	6	58	.272	282	376	21	.969
1953—Brooklyn	Nat.	SS	140	524	108	142	25	7	13	61	.271	265	380	23	.966
1954—Brooklyn	Nat.	SS	141	554	98	171	35	8	10	69	.309	270	426	25	.965
1955—Brooklyn	Nat.	SS	145	553	99	156	29	4	10	61	.282	239	404	23	.965
1956—Brooklyn	Nat.	SS-3B	147	572	85	147	19	2	9	46	.257	269	388	25	.963
1957—Brooklyn	Nat.	3B-SS	103	330	33	74	3	1	1	29	.224	97	228	19	.945
1958—Los Angeles	Nat.	SS-3B	59	147	21	33	7	2	4	17	.224	44	89	10	.930
Major League Totals			2166	8058	1338	2170	330	80	126	885	.269	4124	6131	407	.962

WORLD SERIES RECORD

Year Club	League	Pos.	G.	AB.	R.	H.	2B.	3B.	HR.	RBI.	B.A.	PO.	A.	E.	F.A.
1941—Brooklyn	Nat.	SS	5	20	1	4	0	0	0	2	.200	13	14	3	.900
1947—Brooklyn	Nat.	SS	7	23	5	7	1	0	0	4	.304	8	15	1	.958
1949—Brooklyn	Nat.	SS	5	19	2	6	1	0	1	2	.316	5	9	1	.933
1952—Brooklyn	Nat.	SS	7	29	4	10	0	0	1	4	.345	15	18	2	.943
1953—Brooklyn	Nat.	SS	6	24	0	5	0	1	0	0	.278	7	14	0	1.000
1955—Brooklyn	Nat.	SS	7	27	5	8	1	0	0	2	.296	15	23	1	.974
1956—Brooklyn	Nat.	SS	7	27	3	6	0	1	0	2	.222	14	21	1	.972
World Series Totals			44	169	20	46	3	2	2	16	.272	77	114	9	.955

Marty Marion

Year Club	League	Pos.	G.	AB.	R.	H.	2B.	3B.	HR.	RBI.	B.A.	PO.	A.	E.	F.A.
1936—Huntington	Mid-Atl.	SS	130	511	80	137	26	3	9	75	.268	268	415	54	.927
1937—Rochester	Int.	SS	142	479	73	118	21	3	4	37	.246	249	408	47	.933
1938—Rochester	Int.	SS	109	337	32	84	15	2	2	21	.249	153	258	14	.967
1939—Rochester	Int.	SS	128	437	66	119	12	5	5	53	.272	281	366	40	.942
1940—St. Louis	Nat.	SS	125	435	44	121	18	1	3	46	.278	245	366	33	.949
1941—St. Louis	Nat.	SS	155	547	50	138	22	3	3	58	.252	299	489	38	.954
1942—St. Louis	Nat.	SS	147	485	66	134	38	5	0	54	.276	296	448	31	.960
1943—St. Louis	Nat.	SS	129	418	38	117	15	3	1	52	.280	232	424	20	.970
1944—St. Louis	Nat.	SS	144	506	50	135	26	2	6	63	.267	268	461	21	.972
1945—St. Louis	Nat.	SS	123	430	63	119	27	5	1	59	.277	237	372	21	.967
1946—St. Louis	Nat.	SS	146	498	51	116	29	4	3	46	.233	290	480	21	.973
1947—St. Louis	Nat.	SS	149	540	57	147	19	6	4	74	.272	329	452	15	.981
1948—St. Louis	Nat.	SS	144	567	70	143	26	4	4	43	.252	263	445	19	.974
1949—St. Louis	Nat.	SS	134	515	61	140	31	2	5	70	.272	242	441	17	.976
1950—St. Louis	Nat.	SS	106	372	36	92	10	2	4	40	.247	180	313	11	.978
1951—St. Louis	Nat.						(Did not play)								
1952—St. Louis	Amer.	SS	67	186	16	46	11	0	2	19	.247	105	138	5	.980
1953—St. Louis	Amer.	3B	3	7	0	0	0	0	0	0	.000	1	0	0	1.000
National League Totals			1502	5313	586	1402	261	37	34	605	.264	2881	4691	247	.968
American League Totals			70	193	16	46	11	0	2	19	.238	106	138	5	.980
Major League Totals			1572	5506	602	1448	272	37	36	624	.263	2987	4829	252	.969

WORLD SERIES RECORD

Year Club	League	Pos.	G.	AB	R.	H.	2B.	3B.	HR.	RBI.	B.A.	PO.	A.	E.	F.A.
1942—St. Louis	Nat.	SS	5	18	2	2	0	1	0	3	.111	13	16	0	1.000
1943—St. Louis	Nat.	SS	5	14	1	5	2	0	1	2	.357	8	14	1	.957
1944—St. Louis	Nat.	SS	6	22	1	5	3	0	0	2	.227	7	22	0	1.000
1946—St. Louis	Nat.	SS	7	24	1	6	2	0	0	4	.250	12	22	2	.944
World's Series Totals			23	78	5	18	7	1	1	11	.231	40	74	3	.974

Ernie Banks

Year Club	League	Pos.	G.	AB.	R.	H.	2B.	3B.	HR.	RBI.	B.A.	PO.	A.	E.	F.A.
1953—Chicago	Nat.	SS	10	35	3	11	1	1	2	6	.314	19	33	1	.981
1954—Chicago	Nat.	SS	154	593	70	163	19	7	19	79	.275	312	475	34	.959
1955—Chicago	Nat.	SS	154	596	98	176	29	9	44	117	.295	290	482	22	.972
1956—Chicago	Nat.	SS	139	538	82	160	25	8	28	85	.297	279	357	25	.962
1957—Chicago	Nat.	SS-3B	156	594	113	169	34	6	43	102	.285	241	348	14	.977
1958—Chicago	Nat.	SS	154	617	119	193	23	11	47	129	.313	292	468	32	.960
1959—Chicago	Nat.	SS	155	589	97	179	25	6	45	143	.304	271	519	12	.985
1960—Chicago	Nat.	SS	156	597	94	162	32	7	41	117	.271	283	488	18	.977
1961—Chicago	Nat.	SS-OF-1B	138	511	75	142	22	4	29	80	.278	273	370	21	.968
1962—Chicago	Nat.	1B-3B	154	610	87	164	20	6	37	104	.269	1462	107	11	.993
1963—Chicago	Nat.	1B	130	432	41	98	20	1	18	64	.227	1178	78	9	.993
1964—Chicago	Nat.	1B	157	591	67	156	29	6	23	95	.264	1565	132	10	.994
1965—Chicago	Nat.	1B	163	612	79	162	25	3	28	106	.265	1682	93	15	.992
1966—Chicago	Nat.	1B-3B	141	511	52	139	23	7	15	75	.272	1183	92	13	.990
1967—Chicago	Nat.	1B	151	573	68	158	26	4	23	95	.276	1383	91	10	.993
1968—Chicago	Nat.	1B	150	552	71	136	27	0	32	83	.246	1379	88	6	.996
1969—Chicago	Nat.	1B	155	565	60	143	19	2	23	106	.253	1419	87	4	.997
1970—Chicago	Nat.	1B	72	222	25	56	6	2	12	44	.252	528	35	4	.993
1971—Chicago	Nat.	1B	39	83	4	16	2	0	3	6	.193	167	12	0	1.000
Major League Totals			2528	9421	1305	2583	407	90	512	1636	.274	14206	4355	261	.986

Luis Aparicio

Year Club	League	Pos.	G.	AB.	R.	H.	2B.	3B.	HR.	RBI.	B.A.	PO.	A.	E.	F.A.
1954—Waterloo	I.I.I.	SS	94	390	85	110	18	4	4	47	.282	220	275	31	.941
1955—Memphis	South.	SS	150	564	92	154	24	3	6	51	.273	314	433	44	.944
1956—Chicago	Amer.	SS	152	533	69	142	19	6	3	56	.266	250	474	35	.954
1957—Chicago	Amer.	SS	143	575	82	148	22	6	3	41	.257	246	449	20	.972
1958—Chicago	Amer.	SS	145	557	76	148	20	9	2	40	.266	289	463	21	.973
1959—Chicago	Amer.	SS	152	612	98	157	18	5	6	51	.257	282	460	23	.970
1960—Chicago	Amer.	SS	153	600	86	166	20	7	2	61	.277	305	551	18	.979
1961—Chicago	Amer.	SS	156	625	90	170	24	4	6	45	.272	264	487	30	.962
1962—Chicago(a)	Amer.	SS	153	581	72	140	23	5	7	40	.241	280	452	20	.973
1963—Baltimore	Amer.	SS	146	601	73	150	18	8	5	45	.250	275	403	12	.983
1964—Baltimore	Amer.	SS	146	578	93	154	20	3	10	37	.266	260	437	15	.979
1965—Baltimore	Amer.	SS	144	564	67	127	20	10	8	40	.225	238	439	20	.971
1966—Baltimore	Amer.	SS	151	659	97	182	25	8	6	41	.276	303	441	17	.978
1967—Baltimore(b)	Amer.	SS	134	546	55	127	22	5	4	31	.233	221	333	25	.957
1968—Chicago	Amer.	SS	155	622	55	164	24	4	4	36	.264	269	535	19	.977
1969—Chicago	Amer.	SS	156	599	77	168	24	5	5	51	.280	248	563	20	.976
1970—Chicago(c)	Amer.	SS	146	552	86	173	29	3	5	43	.313	251	483	18	.976
1971—Boston	Amer.	SS	125	491	56	114	23	0	4	45	.232	194	338	16	.971
1972—Boston	Amer.	SS	110	436	47	112	26	3	3	39	.257	183	304	16	.968
1973—Boston	Amer.	SS	132	499	56	135	17	1	0	49	.271	190	404	21	.966
Major League Totals			2599	10230	1335	2677	394	92	83	791	.262	4548	8016	366	.971

WORLD SERIES RECORD

Year Club	League	Pos.	G.	AB.	R.	H.	2B.	3B.	HR.	RBI.	B.A.	PO.	A.	E.	F.A.
1959—Chicago	Amer.	SS	6	26	1	8	1	0	0	0	.308	10	16	2	.929
1966—Baltimore	Amer.	SS	4	16	0	4	1	0	0	2	.250	9	8	0	1.000
World Series Totals			10	42	1	12	2	0	0	2	.286	19	24	2	.956

Dave Concepcion

Year Club	League	Pos.	G.	AB.	R.	H.	2B.	3B.	HR.	RBI.	B.A.	PO.	A.	E.	F.A.
1968—Tampa	Fla. St.	SS-2B	120	329	47	77	11	1	0	22	.234	151	239	20	.951
1969—Asheville	South.	SS	96	340	47	100	11	5	1	37	.294	157	292	29	.939
1969—Indianapolis	A.A.	S-2-3-O	42	167	29	57	7	1	0	17	.341	76	128	9	.958
1970—Cincinnati	Nat.	SS-2B	101	265	38	69	6	3	1	19	.260	144	247	22	.947
1971—Cincinnati	Nat.	S2-3-O	130	327	24	67	4	4	1	20	.205	182	310	13	.974
1972—Cincinnati	Nat.	SS-3B-2B	119	378	40	79	13	2	2	29	.209	197	372	19	.968
1973—Cincinnati	Nat.	SS-OF	89	328	39	94	18	3	8	46	.287	167	292	12	.975
1974—Cincinnati	Nat.	SS-OF	160	594	70	167	25	1	14	82	.281	239	536	30	.963
1975—Cincinnati	Nat.	SS-3B	140	507	62	139	23	1	5	49	.274	241	446	16	.977
1976—Cincinnati	Nat.	SS	152	576	74	162	28	7	9	69	.281	304	506	27	.968
1977—Cincinnati	Nat.	SS	156	572	59	155	26	3	8	64	.271	280	490	11	.986
1978—Cincinnati	Nat.	SS	153	565	75	170	33	4	6	67	.301	255	459	23	.969
1979—Cincinnati	Nat.	SS	149	590	91	166	25	3	16	84	.281	284	495	27	.967
1980—Cincinnati	Nat.	SS-2B	156	622	72	162	31	8	5	77	.260	265	451	16	.978
1981—Cincinnati	Nat.	SS	106	421	57	129	28	0	5	67	.306	208	322	22	.960
1982—Cincinnati	Nat.	SS-1B-3B	147	572	48	164	25	4	5	53	.287	271	459	17	.977
1983—Cincinnati	Nat.	SS-3B-1B	143	528	54	123	22	0	1	47	.233	227	387	13	.979
1984—Cincinnati	Nat.	SS-3B-1B	154	531	46	130	26	1	4	58	.245	213	324	17	.969
1985—Cincinnati	Nat.	SS-3B	155	560	59	141	19	2	7	48	.252	214	405	24	.963
1986—Cincinnati	Nat.	S-1-2-3	90	311	42	81	13	2	3	30	.260	153	223	10	.974
1987—Cincinnati	Nat.	2-1-3-S	104	279	32	89	15	0	1	33	.319	250	169	5	.988
1988—Cincinnati	Nat.	2-1-S-3-P	84	197	11	39	9	0	0	8	.198	151	131	2	.993
Major League Totals—19 Years			2488	8723	993	2326	389	48	101	950	.267	4245	7024	326	.972

CHAMPIONSHIP SERIES RECORD

Year Club	League	Pos.	G.	AB.	R.	H.	2B.	3B.	HR.	RBI.	B.A.	PO.	A.	E.	F.A.
1970—Cincinnati	Nat.	PR-SS	3	0	0	0	0	0	0	0	.000	1	1	0	1.000
1972—Cincinnati	Nat.	PH-S-PR	3	2	0	0	0	0	0	0	.000	0	0	0	.000
1975—Cincinnati	Nat.	SS	3	11	2	5	0	0	1	1	.455	6	8	1	.933
1976—Cincinnati	Nat.	SS	3	10	4	2	1	0	0	0	.200	2	12	0	1.000
1979—Cincinnati	Nat.	SS	3	14	1	6	1	0	0	0	.429	3	14	0	1.000
Championship Series Totals—5 Years			15	37	7	13	2	0	1	1	.351	12	35	1	.979

WORLD SERIES RECORD

Year Club	League	Pos.	G.	AB.	R.	H.	2B.	3B.	HR.	RBI.	B.A.	PO.	A.	E.	F.A.
1970—Cincinnati	Nat.	SS	3	9	0	3	0	1	0	3	.333	2	2	0	1.000
1972—Cincinnati	Nat.	S-PR-PH	6	13	2	4	0	1	0	2	.308	4	11	1	.938
1975—Cincinnati	Nat.	SS	7	28	3	5	1	0	1	4	.179	12	22	1	.971
1976—Cincinnati	Nat.	SS	4	14	1	5	1	1	0	3	.357	6	11	1	.944
World Series Totals—4 Years			20	64	6	17	2	3	1	12	.266	24	46	3	.959

Robin Yount

Year Club	League	Pos.	G.	AB.	R.	H.	2B.	3B.	HR.	RBI.	B.A.	PO.	A.	E.	F.A.
1973—Newark	NYP	SS	64	242	29	69	15	3	3	25	.285	43	85	18	.877
1974—Milwaukee	Amer.	SS	107	344	48	86	14	5	3	26	.250	148	327	19	.962
1975—Milwaukee	Amer.	SS	147	558	67	149	28	2	8	52	.267	273	402	44	.939
1976—Milwaukee	Amer.	SS-OF	161	638	59	161	19	3	2	54	.252	290	510	31	.963
1977—Milwaukee	Amer.	SS	154	605	66	174	34	4	4	49	.288	256	449	29	.964
1978—Milwaukee	Amer.	SS	127	502	66	147	23	9	9	71	.293	246	453	30	.959
1979—Milwaukee	Amer.	SS	149	577	72	154	26	5	8	51	.267	267	517	25	.969
1980—Milwaukee	Amer.	SS	143	611	121	179	49	10	23	87	.293	239	455	28	.961
1981—Milwaukee	Amer.	SS	96	377	50	103	15	5	10	49	.273	161	370	8	.985
1982—Milwaukee	Amer.	SS	156	635	129	210	46	12	29	114	.331	253	489	24	.969
1983—Milwaukee	Amer.	SS	149	578	102	178	42	10	17	80	.308	256	420	19	.973
1984—Milwaukee	Amer.	SS	160	624	105	186	27	7	16	80	.298	199	402	18	.971
1985—Milwaukee	Amer.	OF-1B	122	466	76	129	26	3	15	68	.277	267	5	8	.971
1986—Milwaukee	Amer.	OF-1B	140	522	82	163	31	7	9	46	.312	365	9	2	.995
1987—Milwaukee	Amer.	OF	158	635	99	198	25	9	21	103	.312	380	5	5	.987
1988—Milwaukee	Amer.	OF	162	621	92	190	38	11	13	91	.306	444	12	2	.996
1989—Milwaukee	Amer.	OF	160	614	101	195	38	9	21	103	.318	361	8	7	.981
1990—Milwaukee	Amer.	OF	158	587	98	145	17	5	17	77	.247	422	3	4	.991
Major League Totals—17 Years			2449	9494	1433	2747	498	116	225	1201	.289	4827	4836	300	.970

DIVISION SERIES RECORD

Year Club	League	Pos.	G.	AB.	R.	H.	2B.	3B.	HR.	RBI.	B.A.	PO.	A.	E.	F.A.
1981—Milwaukee	Amer.	SS	5	19	4	6	0	1	0	1	.316	6	16	1	.957

CHAMPIONSHIP SERIES RECORD

Year Club	League	Pos.	G.	AB.	R.	H.	2B.	3B.	HR.	RBI.	B.A.	PO.	A.	E.	F.A.
1982—Milwaukee	Amer.	SS	5	16	1	4	0	0	0	0	.250	11	12	1	.958

WORLD SERIES RECORD

Shares World Series record for most-at-bats, nine-inning game (6), October 12, 1982.

Year Club	League	Pos.	G.	AB.	R.	H.	2B.	3B.	HR.	RBI.	B.A.	PO.	A.	E.	F.A.
1982—Milwaukee	Amer.	SS	7	29	6	12	3	0	1	6	.414	20	19	3	.929

Alan Trammell

Year Club	League	Pos.	G.	AB.	R.	H.	2B.	3B.	HR.	RBI.	B.A.	PO.	A.	E.	F.A.
1976—Bristol	Appal.	SS	41	140	27	38	2	2	0	7	.271	59	131	12	.941
1976—Montgomery	South.	SS	21	56	4	10	0	0	0	2	.179	40	64	2	.981
1977—Montgomery	South.	SS	134	454	78	132	9	19	3	50	.291	188	397	27	.956
1977—Detroit	Amer.	SS	19	43	6	8	0	0	0	0	.186	15	34	2	.961
1978—Detroit	Amer.	SS	139	448	49	120	14	6	2	34	.268	239	421	14	.979
1979—Detroit	Amer.	SS	142	460	68	127	11	4	6	50	.276	245	388	26	.961
1980—Detroit	Amer.	SS	146	560	107	168	21	5	9	65	.300	225	412	13	.980
1981—Detroit	Amer.	SS	105	392	52	101	15	3	2	31	.258	181	347	9	.983
1982—Detroit	Amer.	SS	157	489	66	126	34	3	9	57	.258	259	459	16	.978
1983—Detroit	Amer.	SS	142	505	83	161	31	2	14	66	.319	236	367	13	.979
1984—Detroit	Amer.	SS	139	555	85	174	34	5	14	69	.314	180	314	10	.980
1985—Detroit	Amer.	SS	149	605	79	156	21	7	13	57	.258	225	400	15	.977
1986—Detroit	Amer.	SS	151	574	107	159	33	7	21	75	.277	238	445	22	.969
1987—Detroit	Amer.	SS	151	597	109	205	34	3	28	105	.343	222	421	19	.971
1988—Detroit	Amer.	SS	128	466	73	145	24	1	15	69	.311	195	355	11	.980
1989—Detroit	Amer.	SS	121	449	54	109	20	3	5	43	.243	188	396	9	.985
1990—Detroit	Amer.	SS	146	559	71	170	37	1	14	89	.304	232	409	14	.979
Major League Totals—14 Years			1835	6702	1009	1929	329	50	152	810	.288	2880	5168	193	.977

CHAMPIONSHIP SERIES RECORD

Year Club	League	Pos.	G.	AB.	R.	H.	2B.	3B.	HR.	RBI.	B.A.	PO.	A.	E.	F.A.
1984—Detroit	Amer.	SS	3	11	2	4	0	1	1	3	.364	1	8	0	1.000
1987—Detroit	Amer.	SS	5	20	3	4	1	0	0	2	.200	6	9	1	.938
Championship Series Totals—2 Years			8	31	5	8	1	1	1	5	.258	7	17	1	.960

WORLD SERIES RECORD

Year Club	League	Pos.	G.	AB.	R.	H.	2B.	3B.	HR.	RBI.	B.A.	PO.	A.	E.	F.A.
1984—Detroit	Amer.	SS	5	20	5	9	1	0	2	6	.450	8	9	1	.944

Ozzie Smith

Year Club	League	Pos.	G.	AB.	R.	H.	2B.	3B.	HR.	RBI.	B.A.	PO.	A.	E.	F.A.
1977—Walla Walla	N'west	SS	68	287	69	87	10	2	1	35	.303	130	254	23	.943
1978—San Diego	Nat.	SS	159	590	69	152	17	6	1	46	.258	264	548	25	.970
1979—San Diego	Nat.	SS	156	587	77	124	18	6	0	27	.211	256	555	20	.976
1980—San Diego	Nat.	SS	158	609	67	140	18	5	0	35	.230	288	621	24	.974
1981—San Diego	Nat.	SS	110	450	53	100	11	2	0	21	.222	220	422	16	.976
1982—St. Louis	Nat.	SS	140	488	58	121	24	1	2	43	.248	279	535	13	.984
1983—St. Louis	Nat.	SS	159	552	69	134	30	6	3	50	.243	304	519	21	.975
1984—St. Louis	Nat.	SS	124	412	53	106	20	5	1	44	.257	233	437	12	.982
1985—St. Louis	Nat.	SS	158	537	70	148	22	3	6	54	.276	264	549	14	.983
1986—St. Louis	Nat.	SS	153	514	67	144	19	4	0	54	.280	229	453	15	.978
1987—St. Louis	Nat.	SS	158	600	104	182	40	4	0	75	.303	245	516	10	.987
1988—St. Louis	Nat.	SS	153	575	80	155	27	1	3	51	.270	234	519	22	.972
1989—St. Louis	Nat.	SS	155	593	82	162	30	8	2	50	.273	209	483	17	.976
1990—St. Louis	Nat.	SS	143	512	61	130	21	1	1	50	.254	212	378	12	.980
Major League Totals—13 Years			1926	7019	910	1798	297	52	19	600	.256	3237	6535	221	.978

CHAMPIONSHIP SERIES RECORD

Year Club	League	Pos.	G.	AB.	R.	H.	2B.	3B.	HR.	RBI.	B.A.	PO.	A.	E.	F.A.
1982—St. Louis	Nat.	SS	3	9	0	5	0	0	0	3	.556	4	11	0	1.000
1985—St. Louis	Nat.	SS	6	23	4	10	1	1	1	3	.435	6	16	0	1.000
1987—St. Louis	Nat.	SS	7	25	2	5	0	1	0	1	.200	10	19	1	.967
Championship Series Totals—3 Years			16	57	6	20	1	2	1	7	.351	20	46	1	.985

WORLD SERIES RECORD

Year Club	League	Pos.	G.	AB.	R.	H.	2B.	3B.	HR.	RBI.	B.A.	PO.	A.	E.	F.A.
1982—St. Louis	Nat.	SS	7	24	3	5	0	0	0	1	.208	22	17	0	1.000
1985—St. Louis	Nat.	SS	7	23	1	2	0	0	0	0	.087	10	16	1	.963
1987—St. Louis	Nat.	SS	7	28	3	6	0	0	0	2	.214	7	19	0	1.000
World Series Totals—3 Years			21	75	7	13	0	0	0	3	.173	39	52	1	.989

Cal Ripkin, Jr.

Year Club	League	Pos.	G.	AB.	R.	H.	2B.	3B.	HR.	RBI.	B.A	PO.	A.	E.	F.A.
1978—Bluefield	Appal.	SS	63	239	27	63	7	1	0	24	.264	92	204	33	.900
1979—Miami	Fla. St.	3B-SS-2B	105	393	51	119	28	1	5	54	.303	149	260	30	.932
1979—Charlotte	South.	3B	17	61	6	11	0	1	3	8	.180	13	26	3	.929
1980—Charlotte	South.	3B-SS	144	522	91	144	28	5	25	78	.276	151	341	35	.934
1981—Rochester	Int.	3B-SS	114	437	74	126	31	4	23	75	.288	128	320	21	.955
1981—Baltimore	Amer.	SS-3B	23	39	1	5	0	0	0	0	.128	13	30	3	.935
1982—Baltimore	Amer.	SS-3B	160	598	90	158	32	5	28	93	.264	221	440	19	.972
1983—Baltimore	Amer.	SS	162	663	121	211	47	2	27	102	.318	272	534	25	.970
1984—Baltimore	Amer.	SS	162	641	103	195	37	7	27	86	.304	297	583	26	.971
1985—Baltimore	Amer.	SS	161	642	116	181	32	5	26	110	.282	286	474	26	.967
1986—Baltimore	Amer.	SS	162	627	98	177	35	1	25	81	.282	240	482	13	.982
1987—Baltimore	Amer.	SS	162	624	97	157	28	3	27	98	.252	240	480	20	.973
1988—Baltimore	Amer.	SS	161	575	87	152	25	1	23	81	.264	284	480	21	.973
1989—Baltimore	Amer.	SS	162	646	80	166	30	0	21	93	.257	276	531	8	.990
1990—Baltimore	Amer.	SS	161	600	78	150	28	4	21	84	.250	242	435	3	.996
Major League Totals—10 Years			1476	5655	871	1552	294	28	225	828	.274	2371	4469	164	.977

CHAMPIONSHIP SERIES RECORD

Year Club	League	Pos.	G.	AB.	R.	H.	2B.	3B.	HR.	RBI.	B.A.	PO.	A.	E.	F.A.
1983—Baltimore	Amer.	SS	4	15	5	6	2	0	0	1	.400	7	11	0	1.000

WORLD SERIES RECORD

Year Club	League	Pos.	G.	AB.	R.	H.	2B.	3B.	HR.	RBI.	B.A.	PO.	A.	E.	F.A.
1983—Baltimore	Amer	SS	5	18	2	3	0	0	0	1	.167	6	14	0	.1000

INDEX

Order Directly from the Elysian Fields Press's Fabulous Roster of Baseball Books

This Season's Outstanding New Entries

☐ **THE GINGER KID: The Buck Weaver Story**
by Irving M. Stein

Ship Date: March 1992/ISBN: 0–697–16276–1/272 pages/$19.95

Was Buck Weaver a crook or a martyr? Did he betray baseball and his fans by "selling out" in the infamous Black Sox scandal of 1919, or did organized baseball destroy the career of an innocent man who played the game with great skill, passion, and joy? Is it a crime or a virtue to refuse to "rat" on your friends and comrades? This moving biography of a pivotal player in baseball lore reveals unknown facts about the circumstances surrounding the time—over 70 years ago—when men conspired to lose a World Series in exchange for monetary gain.

☐ **IN THE SHADOWS OF THE DIAMOND: Hard Times in the National Pastime**
by James Costello and Michael Santa Maria

Ship Date: March 1992/ISBN: 0–697–15031–3/288 pages/$19.95

Thoroughly researched, this lively and fascinating collection of historical vignettes reveals the truth behind the legendary baseball tales of fateful accident and astonishing triumph, untimely deaths and miraculous comebacks, boneheads, victims of unfortunate circumstances, and tragically flawed heros. By presenting the complete facts and full historical context surrounding the players and incidents, this book exonerates ball players who have been unfairly condemned by a single event in their careers and indicts others who have somehow escaped historical judgement.

☐ **THE ALL-TIME ALL-STARS BASEBALL BOOK: The Greatest, Oddest, and Worst Lineups in the History of the National Pastime**
by Donald Dewey and Nick Acocella

Ship Date: March 1992/ISBN: 0–697–14594–8/272 pages (paper)/ $10.95

Once a baseball fan starts reading this book, he or she won't be able to stop. From the best ever (by position) in World Series play to the All-Fish team (with every position represented), from the greatest (by position) to ever wear the uniform of the New York Yankees to the absolute worst hitters (by position) in major league history, this delightful encyclopedia of lineups is brimming with astounding little-known baseball facts and arcana. But it offers much more than that. It is also a charmingly eccentric ramble through baseball anecdote and record, a quirky sort of historical document, providing the reader with a highly entertaining education in the strange and wonderful world of organized baseball. And it's all centered around the simplest and most direct format baseball has to offer: the lineup card.

☐ **1992 BASEBALL SABERMETRIC**
by Brock Hanke

Ship Date: March 1992/ISBN: 0–697–16612–0/320 pages (8½ × 11, paper)/$15.95

The only true successor to the *Baseball Abstract*. This book maintains the format and statistical approach of the *Bill James Baseball Abstracts* of the 1980s. It is filled with irreverent and witty team essays, player rankings, and studies that are at the cutting edge of baseball analysis. *Baseball Sabermetric* is the only book applying Bill James' formulas and is the current forerunner in baseball statistical analysis. It features the best statistical presentation in the field courtesy of Stats, Inc. and is recommended by *Baseball America*. Includes rotisserie best and worst buys.

A Terrific Line Up of Baseball Books Still Available from the Elysian Fields Press

☐ **THE LAST .400 HITTER**
by John B. Holway

1991/304 pages/Cloth/ISBN 14129/$19.95

In the Summer of 1941 Ted Williams and Joe DiMaggio stood at the most dramatic peaks of their lives. DiMaggio created a legend in the best two months he ever played. Williams reached a height that no other man has scaled in 60 years. John B. Holway tells us the story about the famous last .400 hitter—Ted Williams.

☐ **THE GREATEST CATCHERS OF ALL TIME**
by Don Honig

1991/160 pages/Cloth/ISBN 12806/$18.95

A one-of-akind book—a one-of-akind series. In this unique book, Donald Honig highlights the careers of the 15 greatest catchers of all time.

☐ **THE PITTSBURGH CRAWFORDS: The Lives & Times of Black Baseball's Most Exciting Team**
by Jim Bankes

1991/195 pages/Paper/ISBN 12889/$15.95

A tribute to the most talented team in the National Negro League during the '30s: the Pittsburgh Crawfords.

☐ **BASEBALL BY THE BOOKS**
by Andy McCue

1990/175 pages/Paper/ISBN 12764/$19.95

If you love baseball and love reading about it even more, this book is a must for you! For over three years, Andy McCue has researched, gathered, and compiled over 1,300 entries in his new baseball fiction bibliography.

☐ **TEACHING THE MENTAL ASPECTS OF BASEBALL: A Coach's Handbook**
by Al Figone, Humboldt State University

1990/240 pages/Paper/ISBN 12767/$15.95

At last! A practical book for coaches and players of all levels about integrating the mental aspects of baseball when executing the technical skills.

☐ **BUILDING A BETTER HITTER**
by Stephen Pecci; Foreword by George Foster

1990/112 pages/Paper/ISBN 11404/$10.95

There's more to successful hitting than just good swings. Pecci's new book provides coaches and players with a program that produces better hitters.

☐ **THE COMPLETE BASEBALL HANDBOOK: Strategies and Techniques for Winning**
by Walter Alston and Don Weiskopf

1984/530 pages/Paper/ISBN 6819/$16.95

Drawing upon 23 years of experience as manager of the Brooklyn/L.A. Dodgers—seven league pennants, and four World Series Championships—the late Walter Alston's time-honored philosophy on both the basics and fine points of coaching is geared toward producing better ball players and winning teams!

ORDER FORM

TO ORDER ANY OR ALL OF THESE TITLES:

1. **CALL Toll Free 1–800–338–5578**

2. Send check or money order plus appropriate state tax and $1.00 shipping and handling for each book ordered along with a list of the books you would like to receive (include ISBN numbers) to:

> Wm. C. Brown Publishers
> 2460 Kerper Boulevard
> Dubuque, Iowa 52001

SHIP TO: _____ BOOK TOTAL $ _____

_____ TAX $ _____

City _____ State ____ Zip ____ SHIPPING $ _____

TOTAL $ _____

REMEMBER TO ASK FOR A **FREE** CATALOG LISTING ALL OF OUR COACHING TITLES